Praise for
Charleston's Old Exchange Building
A Witness to American History

"If these walls could talk, what wonderful stories they could tell!" We often say this of historic buildings. Charleston's Exchange needs no voice, however—for authors Ruth Miller and Ann Andrus do the job expertly. In dramatic vignettes they interpret not just the history of one of America's grand buildings, but also the history of one of America's grand cities. The building serves as a window affording us grand and glorious glimpses of Charleston's past. Recommended!

Harlan Greene
Historian and Charleston author

In *Charleston's Old Exchange*, Ruth M. Miller and Ann T. Andrus have skillfully brought to life the rich history of one of American's most important buildings.

W. Eric Emerson, PhD
Executive Director, South Carolina Historical Society

This is a lively, interesting and accurate little book about one of Charleston's most important and historic buildings, the Old Exchange. The illustrations, photographs and quotations from original sources all contribute to a full and picturesque portrait of a singular building.

Robert N. Rosen
Author of *A Short History of Charleston*

Charleston's Old Exchange Building

A Witness to American History

Ruth M. Miller
Ann Taylor Andrus

CHARLESTON · LONDON
History
PRESS

Published by The History Press
18 Percy Street
Charleston, SC 29403
866.223.5778
www.historypress.net

Copyright © 2005 by Ann Taylor Andrus and Ruth M. Miller
All rights reserved

Cover: The Exchange Building was a center of activity on Charleston's waterfront. *From a reproduction of a painting by Gil Petroff, courtesy of the Old Exchange and Provost Dungeon.*

First published 1986
The History Press edition 2005

Manufactured in the United Kingdom

ISBN 1.59629.046.3

Library of Congress Cataloging-in-Publication Data

Andrus, Ann Taylor.
  Charleston's Old Exchange Building : a witness to American history / Ann Taylor Andrus and Ruth M. Miller.
      p. cm.
  Includes bibliographical references and index.
  ISBN 1-59629-046-3 (alk. paper)
  1. Old Exchange Building and Provost Dungeon (Charleston, S.C.) 2. Historic buildings--South Carolina--Charleston. 3. Charleston (S.C.)--Buildings, structures, etc. 4. Charleston (S.C.)--History. 5. Charleston (S.C.)--Commerce--History. I. Miller, Ruth M., 1943- II. Title.
  F279.C48O434 2005
  975.7'915--dc22
                         2005016590

Contents

Acknowledgements

The authors acknowledge with gratitude the assistance offered by the following when producing the first edition of this book: Mr. and Mrs. Charles N. Bayless, Harrington Bissell, Mrs. Joyce Ellis, Ernestine C. Fellers, Elizabeth Verner Hamilton, Mrs. Thomas Hutto, Alice Levkof, Jack Mitchell, Mr. and Mrs. J.V. Nielsen Jr., Katherine Nicholson, Mrs. Nancy Pinckney, Mrs. Armine Richardson and Robert P. Stockton, as well as the staffs of the Charleston Library Society, the Old Exchange, the South Carolina Historical Society and the members of the Old Exchange Building Commission.

Our special appreciation to Gene Waddell and David Moltke-Hansen for reading and offering comments on the original manuscript.

This second edition owes its existence to the Friends of the Old Exchange. Pharen Elaine Johnson, president, showed great foresight recommending programs and projects that enhanced the appreciation of this historic building. The staff of the Old Exchange responded with good humor and competence to our requests. Three individuals, Donn Pittman, Ian MacDonald and Andrew Miller deserve special recognition for their roles in this publication.

Donn Pittman parented this project from beginning to end. He called numerous meetings and addressed details, always working with determination and diligence.

Ian MacDonald has spent untold hours with his computer and camera. He ensured that materials complied with the publisher's requirements.

Finally, thanks to Andrew Miller, who, with his technological expertise and his camera, put it all together.

To everyone involved, we give our sincere thanks.

Introduction

This is a true tale. It is a story of pirates and patriots, taxes and tea, manners and mobs. The following narration is so full of drama that one might think it fictitious, but all the events described here really happened.

What makes this journey into American history unique? Everything that follows relates to 122 East Bay Street, Charleston, South Carolina. This is the record of one of the most significant buildings in America…the Old Exchange.

Modern-day visitors to this historic site remark on the feelings it evokes, from the eerie atmosphere of the Provost Dungeon to the patriotic awareness of America's founding. The walls of the Exchange are silent; but people leave records, and records are the stuff of history. This book is the result of our search into Charleston's past. We invite you to join us on our adventure.

Ann T. Andrus
Ruth M. Miller
Charleston, South Carolina

The Edward Crisp Map of 1704 is the earliest existing map of fortified Charles Town. *Courtesy of Charleston Library Society.*

Colonial Beginnings, 1670–1766

On an unknown date early in April 1670, the ship *Carolina* sailed into what would become Charleston Harbor. The landing marked the end of a long and arduous voyage for the first English settlers to arrive in this area.

The first colonists settled on the west bank of the Ashley River at a site they called Albermarle. The name was soon changed to Charles Town, however, in honor of Charles II. As the settlers studied the landscape, they determined the best location for their town, which was to become the largest port in the colonial South. Within ten years a move was made across the Ashley River to the peninsula. By 1680 the original site had been abandoned and the area had become a plantation. This location can be explored today within the boundaries of Charles Towne Landing State Park.

Once the settlers had chosen a permanent location on the peninsula, they worked hard to build a fortified town. Needing protection from Indians, foreign invasion and pirates, the founders of Charles Town built a walled city. Charles Town was fortunate to have Sir Nathaniel Johnson as governor during the city's construction.

Prior to arriving in Carolina, Johnson had served in European wars and observed fortifications designed by the great military engineer Vauban. It was Johnson who directed the building of Charles Town's walls. Made of brick, the walls formed a trapezoid that enclosed part of the "Grand

Charleston's Old Exchange Building

Modell" of Charles Town. This Grand Modell was the plan for the city, which had been sent from England. Located at strategic points were bastions that projected out and housed defensive cannons. On the Cooper River, at the midpoint of the wall, stood Half-Moon Battery, the only demi-lune in the outline of the walls. Today the only significant remnant of that wall, the site of Half-Moon Battery, can be seen in the basement of the Exchange Building.

The future site of the Exchange stood at the center of civil and maritime life from Charles Town's earliest days. Bay Street was known as Front Street then, for it fronted on the water. The earliest record of the land on which the Exchange stands is dated August 1, 1699.[1]

The lot, "distinguished by the letter B" on the Grand Modell, was granted by the Right Honorable Joseph Blake, proprietor and governor, to Captain Edmund Bellinger. Bellinger obtained all rights to the property, "with the priviledge of hawking, hunting, fishing, and fowling," in return for "erecting and keeping in Repair a sufficient pair of Steirs or Comon Landing Place of the breadth of Eight feet and half wide with bolts, rings, and posts for Comon Use." Blake reserved only the mineral rights for himself: "Except all Royal miners and quarriers of Gems and Precious Stones and one Sixth

Sir Nathaniel Johnson. *Courtesy of Gibbes Museum of Art/Carolina Art Association.*

part of the Oar [ore] of all base mines after the same is Digged and washed and one tenth part of the same when and after Refined."[2]

Located in the midst of Charles Town's thriving port, the waterfront lot appreciated greatly. In 1738, Edmund Bellinger of Ashley River, and his wife Elizabeth, transferred the property to Ebenezar Simmons, merchant of Charles Town. The transaction took place through an Indenture of Lease in which the property, "being a front or Low Water Lott," was rented for one peppercorn until the final sale.[3] On July 25, 1738, the exchange took place for "800 pounds current money."[4] Twenty-nine years later (in 1767), Henry Middleton, John Neufville, Gabriel Manigault and John Savage, "appraisers of the lands...for an Exchange and Custom House," would pay 5,500 pounds to Ebenezar Simmons for the same property.[5]

Although the Exchange was begun almost one hundred years after the first settlers arrived, Lot B on the Grand Modell witnessed the essence of life in the Carolina Lowcountry during the first century. What happened in those early years? What was life in colonial Charles Town like, and what do the records of Lot B reveal?

This detail of a 1739 engraving shows the Half-Moon Battery and Court of Guard with cannons. *Courtesy of Carolina Galleries.*

This etching, published in 1762 in "London Gentlemen's Magazine," is a view of Charleston Harbor showing the sea wall and fortifications. *Courtesy of Carolina Galleries.*

First of all, colonial life was dangerous. There were walls protecting Charles Town from attack, and on Lot B was the Half-Moon Battery, a defensive fortification complete with cannon. Second, Charles Town was a commercial center in the days of sail, serving as the harbor for tremendous numbers of ships. Third, colonial life was relatively civilized, for the earliest extant map, Edward Crisp's of 1704, shows Half-Moon Battery as the location of the Court of Guard. Drawings of the building show a two-story structure described as "The Council Chamber above and the Guard House below."[6]

The Council Chamber, being one of the largest rooms in the city, was used for many public meetings. Numerous folk, from the petty to the infamous, populated the jail below. Among the infamous, one must count the crew of a certain ship's captain.

His name was Stede Bonnet, and his profession was piracy. He came to Charles Town by way of the high seas. Bonnet was one of those puzzles historians will likely never solve. Born in 1688, he married Mary Allamby and became a major in the British Army; he was also a sugar planter and,

most important of all, a "gentleman." In 1717, Bonnet pulled up roots, bought a ship, hired a crew (very unorthodox for a pirate captain) and ventured forth on a new career.

Why did Bonnet go "apyrating"? Speculation includes that he may have been running from a nagging wife, may have gone insane or that the devil got his way. We will probably never know. Whatever his reasons, the gentleman went "apyrating" at the age of twenty-nine. In a little over a year he captured sixteen vessels, sailed with Blackbeard and became renowned as the "Gentleman Pirate." Bonnet was one of many notorious and disruptive freebooters who threatened the trade that was Charles Town's life blood. But he was also one of a breed destined for death.

Pirates were often a problem around Charles Town. They were known to lurk near the busy channel and capture merchant vessels arriving or departing the bustling harbor. Blackbeard, the most fearsome of pirates, had done just that in May of 1718, with Stede Bonnet on board. In less than a week, Blackbeard took nine vessels and kidnapped several important citizens, whom he ransomed for medicines.

As English shipping suffered, more pressure was put on the colonial government of Charles Town to deal with the pirates. It was in such an atmosphere that Governor Robert Johnson decided to take action. Colonel

Stede Bonnet, the "Gentleman Pirate."
Sketch by Emmet Robinson, used by permission of Harrington Bissell.

William Rhett, a proven military hero, was commissioned to go after a "Captain Thomas" on the basis of reports that his ship was careened at the mouth of the Cape Fear River. Colonel Rhett outfitted sloops with guns and men and departed Charles Town. On October 3, 1718, he returned —with Stede Bonnet and crew under arrest.

The crew was imprisoned in the Guard House at the Half-Moon Battery. Major Bonnet, being "a gentleman," was quartered in the house of Marshall Partridge. While awaiting trial, the cunning Bonnet engineered an escape by dressing up in women's clothing. He tried to reach Christopher Moody, another notorious pirate, off Charles Town's bar. Once again, Colonel Rhett was dispatched; and once again he returned with Bonnet. This time the planter-turned-pirate was tried and sentenced to "be hanged by the neck till you are dead." The public hanging took place on December 10, 1718, at White Point, the sand bar at the confluence of the Ashley and Cooper Rivers. Clutching a bouquet of wilted flowers, manacled and "scarce sensible when he came to the place of execution," Stede Bonnet met his maker.[7]

The Old Exchange was also the place of public entertainment. In January 1703, Anthony Ashton, a British actor, playwright and adventurer, landed

Stede Bonnet was captured by Colonel William Rhett and publicly hanged at White Point in 1718. *Sketch by Emmet Robinson, used by permission of Harrington Bissell.*

in Charles Town. Years later he described that arrival into a city "full of Lice, Shame, Poverty, Nakedness, and Hunger: I turn'd Player and Poet and wrote one Play on the Subject of the Country."[8]

Where exactly Ashton performed is not known, but the earliest surviving record of a public entertainment is dated February 17, 1733. The announcement reads,

> *At the Council Chamber on Monday the 26th instant* [an old expression for the current month] *will be a Consort* [concert] *of vocal and instrumental music. Tickets to be had at Mr. Cook's or Mr. Saurean's at 40 s. N.B. None but English and Scotch Songs.*[9]

Thus the first documented location of a performance in Charles Town is at the Council Chamber, and it is not until later that any records mention a theatre building. One can surmise that the Council Chamber room saw many performances and functions.

One of the best descriptions of the colonial waterfront comes from the pen of Dr. Philip Gendron Prioleau, a local physician. The Medical Society of South Carolina commissioned the doctor to set down an eyewitness record of Charles Town's great hurricanes. In writing his history, Prioleau conscientiously recreated the Charles Town waterfront before disaster struck:[10]

> *The town was in a state of fortification...A very strong brick wall, the curtain line* [the sea wall], *extended on the east side of East Bay Street from Roper's warf to the Governor's bridge, at each extremity of which there was a bastion. The wharves were few in number, the most northwardly of which is now owned by Captain John Blake. With the exception of the low stores on the wharves, the vendue store which was opposite Tradd Street, and the Old Guard House, where the Exchange now stands, there was not a house on the east side of East Bay Street, nor was there any land at that time on which one could be erected. The water washed the curtain line from one end to the other, except only in those places where the wharves projected from it.* [11]

Dr. Prioleau continued by describing the tremendous destruction wrought by the great hurricane of 1752. "The warehouses, scale houses, and sheds upon the wharves, with all the goods in them were swept away; the solid parts of the wharves much leveled. All the floating materials of the wharves, warehouses and their contents — navel stores, boards, timber, shingles, staves, canoes, small craft, and barrels, were washed upon under the curtain line."[12] His indication of "naval stores" could have included the pine pitch, tar and turpentine, all used in the maintaining of ships and important exports of Charles Town.

Now compare Prioleau's account with that of an archaeologist more than two hundred years later. Working on the east side of the Exchange during its restoration, Dr. Elaine Herold noted the materials laid down prior to construction of the Exchange Building:

Dr. Elaine Herold, archaeologist, examines the 1979 excavation at the Exchange Building. *Courtesy of the Old Exchange and Provost Dungeon.*

A stratum which contained a large number of barrel hoops, tops and staves, cut pieces of planking, wood shavings, scrap wood, and wooden shingles. This had been preserved, because a substantial amount of pine pitch had been spilled there. In addition to wood, cloth, pieces of leather, feathers, peach pits, peanut shells, watermelon seeds and gourd fragments were found. The nature of the deposit suggested that it resulted from some sort of accident or disaster on the Charleston waterfront.[13]

The discovery so closely matches Prioleau's description of the 1752 hurricane that Dr. Herold suggests that storm was the likely source of the deposit. And so there is new information on colonial Charles Town, for the pitch settled with flotsam and jetsam to preserve clues to the life, goods and even the diet of the period. More than two thousand artifacts were recovered in Dr. Herold's excavation.[14]

Despite the traumas of colonial times, and through major disasters—man-made and natural—the port prospered.

The Exchange, 1766–1772

By the mid-eighteenth century, there were days when three hundred ships could be counted in Charles Town harbor. Goods arrived from around the world; raw materials and agricultural products were the chief exports. Most important of all was the exportation of rice.

So much commercial activity demanded an exchange and custom house worthy of the chief city in the Southern colonies. In 1766, the Commons House of Assembly of the Province petitioned His Majesty's Council for approval of the building's construction—not as a seat for the royal governor, but as a facility for the people of the colony. They chose the most prominent lot in the city of Charles Town for the location—Lot B on the Grand Modell, where stood the Court of Guard. The *South Carolina Gazette* announced in 1767 that plans for an elegant structure, the New Exchange and Custom House, were before His Majesty's Council.[15]

On April 27, 1767, the Commons House of Assembly, the colonial governing body, passed the act which granted to His Majesty 60,000 pounds to build the new Exchange and Custom House. The money was raised by local taxation. Heavy taxes were levied on wine, rum, "white bisket, middling bisket, ship bisket" and flour. Both essentials and luxuries were included in the list of taxable items, an apparent attempt to collect monies from all the citizens who would benefit from the building. A commission was formed to

This conceptual engraving taken from an early map of Charles Town shows the products of the colony. *Courtesy of the South Carolina Historical Society.*

carry out the act, and since the tax was self-imposed, there were no cries of "taxation without representation."[16]

By December the land had been purchased and agreements signed with John and Peter Horlbeck for construction at a cost of "Forty one Thousand Seven Hundred and Forty Pounds lawful Current Money." The Guard House was torn down and the Exchange Building rose on the site. The Horlbecks built what was to become one of the most important structures in colonial America, two others being Independence Hall in Philadelphia and Faneuil Hall in Boston.

Once completed, the Great Hall and rooms on the upper story of the Exchange served as customs offices and an enclosed meeting space. The open arcade on the main floor of the building served as a gathering place for commercial and social activities. The commercial transactions taking place at the Exchange centered on rice, indigo and the slave trade. South Carolina was the major exporter of those plantation-grown crops to England, as well as being the largest importer of slaves among the thirteen colonies.

As demand for foodstuffs and raw materials increased in England, the demand for slaves rose in South Carolina. Close communication between Charles Town merchants and their English counterparts continued as trade shifted and expanded. In 1773, Charles Town exported 59,046,200 pounds of rice and 720,591 pounds of indigo, while importing 6,464 slaves on English ships.[17]

The American Revolution, 1773–1783

The American Revolution rings with taxes and tea; so do the walls of the Exchange. Taxation without representation was a central issue. The colonists felt that the government in Great Britain had no right to levy taxes without colonial consent. There had been arguments over taxation with the Molasses Act of 1733, the Sugar Act of 1764 and the Stamp Act of 1765. In 1767 the Townshend Acts imposed duties on lead, paint, paper, glass and tea. Opposition in the colonies grew as English customs officers tried enforcing each tax. When Lord North of Kirtling became chancellor of the Exchequer in 1770, he suggested that all duties be repealed—except for the tax on tea—to encourage colonial industry. Since tea could not be grown in America, there would be no colonial competition and England would maintain, in principle, her right to tax the colonies. Relative calm reigned on both sides of the Atlantic until 1773.

In that year the Tea Act was passed to help the financially troubled East India Company. Although this law allowed the company to avoid taxes in England and thus lowered the price of tea for Americans, the authority of Parliament to write tax legislation became an issue once more. Taxation without representation was the general issue, but the tax on tea became the focal point.

The first tea chests exported under the Tea Act were sent from London to America's four largest cities: New York, Philadelphia, Boston and Charles

MR. PALMER'S ASSORTMENT OF TEAS FOR AMERICA.

	Boston.	So. Carolina.	New York.	Philadelphia.	Total.
Bohea, l. ch^{ts}	268	182	568	568	1586
Congo, fm'd^0.	20	10	20	20	70
Singlo, d^0.	80	50	80	80	290
Hyfon, d^0.	20	10	20	20	70
Souchong, d^0.	10	5	10	10	35

WEIGHT OF TEA EXPORTED TO AMERICA

	Lbs.
Bohea,	562,421
Singlo,	22,546
Hyfon,	5,285
Souchong,	2,392
Congou,	6,015
Total Lbs	598,659

A list of teas shipped by the East India Company. *From Lipscomb*, South Carolina Becomes a State, *South Carolina Archives.*

Town. What happened in the latter was reported by the *South Carolina Gazette* of December 6, 1773:

> *Last Wednesday evening came in over the bar, the next morning anchored before the town, the ship* London, *Alexander Curling, master from London, with no less than two hundred and fifty seven chests of Tea on board, which were shipped by the East India Company in London…to be received and disposed of in this province, after the payment of a Duty of 3 pence sterling a pound, imposed by the very same act of parliament of G.B…the express purpose of raising a revenue in America, without our consent…Those who thought it would be criminal tamely to give up any of our essential rights as British subjects, and involve our posterity in a state little better than slavery, began to look about them, and to think it high time to contend, legally, and to dispute the assumed power.*[18]

To gain the consensus of the citizens, posters were put up inviting all inhabitants to assemble in the Great Hall over the Exchange. At the meeting an agreement was drawn up not to import any teas with duty. Many signed the document. A committee consisting of Captain Gadsden, Colonel Pinckney, Thomas Ferguson, Charles Cotesworth Pinckney, Esquires; and Mr. Daniel Cannon was sent to visit merchants in town and collect their signatures.[19]

The British customs office was in a quandary. Captain Curling wanted to be rid of the troublesome tea; meanwhile citizens were organizing a rebellion. Very early on December 22, the tea was landed for delivery to the king's officers. All 256 chests were locked up in the cellar of the Exchange, which had been rented for that purpose.[20]

The *Gazette* received, and reported news of what had taken place at other ports where the tea had been sent, and promptly reported to its anxious readership. Since there were no radio or television news reports, everyone waited for the newspaper to announce the latest events around the world. Charlestonians first learned about Boston's Mohawk raiding party, which took place on December 16, 1773, from a *Gazette* article on January 17, 1774:

The East India Company's Tea destined for New York was not arrived there the 27th ult. [the month before] *and the People are said to be determined against its being landed when it does arrive.*

From Philadelphia, where it did arrive, the Ship was sent back for England within 48 Hours, with all the other Goods on board.

And at Boston, on the 16 ult. some Mohawks hoisted out all the Chests that were on board Capt. Hall's and Capt. Bruce's Ships, and Capt. Coffin's Brig, cut them to Pieces, and threw the whole Contents over the Sides of the Water: There were 114 Chests in each vessel: Capt. Loring's Brig, with 58 Chests more, was ashore on the back of Cape Cod. The Bostonians, before they suffered the Mohawks to precede to this Act, finding that no Preparations were making for the Return of those vessels for England, as had been promised, waited until the Expiration of 20 Days, when, to secure the Duties, the Teas were to have been delivered to the Custody of the Man of War by the Collector.

By these Accounts, which we received in Capt. Wright, who arrived here yesterday, from Philadelphia, it appears, that none of the East India Company's Consignments of Tea have yet been landed any where upon this Continent, but here—where it will be found an Article equally unsalable, as if it had been destroyed—without the Company's having their private Property taken from them.

Tea on another ship, this one in Charles Town, met a fate similar to the tea shipped to Boston. At noon on November 3, 1774, seven chests aboard the *Britannia* were dumped into the harbor by the very men to whom they were consigned. The newspaper describes the scene on Captain Ball's ship as an "Oblation to Neptune." A "Committee of Observation" watched on board as merchants broke the chests and emptied the contents into the river. Three hearty cheers were given with the dumping of each chest by the population who watched. The actors were not so dramatic as Boston's Mohawks, but the results were as effective. This was Charles Town's tea party, little remembered but nonetheless noteworthy.

The chests of tea, that had been locked in the Exchange remained there until 1776, when the state of South Carolina declared her independence and took possession of the British tea. On October 14, 1776, Captain Curling's tea was sold for excellent prices to benefit the Revolution. Charles Town not only dumped tea, she profited from it and sipped it as well.[21]

The Great Hall of the Exchange continued to see boisterous mobs, fiery rhetoric and momentous events throughout the Revolution. In July of 1774, the *Gazette* reported on another step toward revolution.

> On Wednesday last, the Sixth Instant, the largest body of the most respectable Inhabitants that had ever been seen together upon any public occasion here, or perhaps anywhere in America met at the Exchange in this Town, in order to consider of the Papers, Letters, and Resolutions that had been transmitted to the said committee from the Northern colonies.[22]

Pressure for an independent government increased. In September 1774, the First Continental Congress assembled in Philadelphia. In May 1775, the Second Continental Congress assumed such governmental functions as establishing a Continental army, appointing George Washington as commander, and issuing currency. In January 1776, a pamphlet called *Common Sense*, which portrayed George III as a tyrant and encouraged Americans to cast off all kings, was printed. On March 28, 1776, South Carolinians wrote a constitution and declared it publicly on the steps of the Exchange. The *South Carolina and American General Gazette* reported the event on April 3, 1776:

> On Thursday last the new Constitution, agreed on by our Congress, by the Approbation of the Continental Congress, "to serve for regulating the internal policy of this Colony until an accommodation of the unhappy Differences between Great Britain and America can be obtained, an event which is earnestly desired" was published here in due form. A Detachment of the Provincial Regiment of Artillery and the Charles Town Militia

Many speakers have been heard in the Great Hall of the Exchange Building.
Sketch by Mary A. Anderson.

*were drawn up in Broad Street from the State House to the Exchange,
where the Constitution was read and the Commissions of John Rutledge,
Esq. President and Commander in Chief, and Henry Laurens, Esq.
Vice President of the Colony, were proclaimed, amidst the Shouts of the
numerous Spectators, Firing of Field Pieces, and the cannon on board the
Provincial armed.*

Thus a republican constitution was written by South Carolina and a
government independent of England was declared at the Exchange. Four
months later the Second Continental Congress in Philadelphia followed South
Carolina's lead, and on July 4, 1776, the Declaration of Independence was
adopted. Eighty-four years later, the citizens of South Carolina, again meeting

John Rutledge, president and commander in chief of the colony of South Carolina. *Courtesy of the South Carolina Historical Society.*

in Charleston, declared their second independence. This time they withdrew from the United States of America. Twice in American history South Carolina led the way to rebellion. Actually, including the bloodless rebellion of 1719, South Carolinians had challenged their government three times by 1860.

When the British occupied Charles Town during the latter part of the American Revolution, they used the basement of the Exchange as a gaol (jail). Unknown to the prisoners, as well as to their British captors, the basement space was shared with a large supply of gunpowder. Years later, General William Moultrie, a local hero of the Revolution, related the story in his memoirs. On Sunday, May 7, 1780,

> *Our principal magazine near being destroyed, by a thirteen inch shell bursting within ten yards of it. The old magazine behind St. Phillip's Church: in consequence of that shell falling so near, I had the powder (10,000 pounds) removed to the north east corner, under the exchange, and had the doors and windows bricked up. Not-withstanding, the British had possession of Charlestown so long, they never discovered the powder, although their provost was the next apartment to it, and after the evacuations, when we came into town, we found the powder as we left it.*[23]

30

General William Moultrie, delegate to the Continental Congress and two-time governor of South Carolina. *Portrait by Charles Fraser, from the City Hall Collection, Charleston, South Carolina.*

Among those who shared the cellars with hidden explosives and common criminals were principal citizens of the state who had been taken from their homes by order of Lord Charles Cornwallis. Daniel Stevens, who was put on board a prison ship (where he became very ill and was later allowed to return home under house arrest) provided a vivid first-person account of confinement in the dank and dark dungeons.[24] "About a month thereafter," he wrote, "the British Provost Master, Jarvis, called at my House early in the morning just after daylight, before I had risen, with an order for me to accompany him to the Town Major, Fraser."

Charged with violating his parole, Stevens continued:

> [I] *was to be closely confined in the Provost in the Cellar under the Exchange, and* [the Commandant] *instantly gave orders to the Provost Sergeant Jarvis to conduct me to that Prison, and that I was there confined by order of the Commandant. It was instantly executed, and I met within the inclosure a number of my friends, who had been previously confined, among them my old friends from the upper Country, Colonels Stark and*

Beard, and Mr. Sheriff Pritchard.

I had not been confined many hours before the Provost Marshall Jarvis returned, with an order that as a violent and refractory character, "that Irons should be placed on my legs and handcuffed." I with firmness of mind desired the Provost Master Jarvis to do his duty, which was done. Jarvis told me he supposed it was done out of revenge, for the message I had sent to the Commandant Balfour "That I despised his threats and would be avenged on him for his violation of my parole, that he was no Soldier, or that he would know how to treat an Officer otherwise."

I made this known to Gen. Greene and after keeping me in Irons near two months, an order was given, and they were re-moved, and a fortnight after, I was released from Prison and returned home and was confined to my house for a short time, and then confined on board a Prison Ship. Not long after, an exchange of 60 prisoners took place between Gen. Greene and the commanding general of the British in South Carolina. And a small party of us who were exchanged chartered a Schooner Carlet and went to Philadelphia.[25]

Another detailed first-person account of life as a prisoner can be found in the diary of Josiah Smith, an important Charles Town merchant. Smith was among those arrested "by order as they said of General Cornwallis, and Felon like, conducted to the upperpart of the Exchange, and there detained under an Officers Guard till about Ten of the Clock, when Boats being provided for their reception, were in them conveyed from thence down to the Armed Ship Sandwich, under command of Capt. William Bett."[26]

In company with Smith on the prison ship were Christopher Gadsden, an outspoken leader in the Revolutionary cause, and two men who distinguished themselves by signing the Declaration of Independence—Thomas Heyward Jr. and Edward Rutledge. Other prominent citizens imprisoned included Richard Hutson, Peter Timothy, John Edwards, William Hazell Gibbes and David Ramsay.[27]

John Milner, a prominent gunsmith, was among those locked in the Provost. An ardent patriot, he had mounted, repaired and fixed guns and other firearms for the Secret Committee as early as 1775. Family papers record that Milner "was imprisoned in the basement of the old post office at the head of Broad Street and East Bay and his Maiden Daughter [Martha] used to feed him through the iron bars or grating with the boiled rice she

Charleston's
Old Exchange Building

East Elevation

West Elevation

1. (Previous pages) William Rigby Naylor's plans of the Exchange Building, dated 1766 and 1767. Note the differences in the riverside elevation, first, and the streetside elevation, second. *Courtesy of the South Carolina Archives.*

2. (Opposite page and above) Thomas Leitch painted this view of the Charles Town waterfront in 1774. It is one of the earliest works that shows the Exchange Building. *Courtesy of the Museum of Early Southern Decorative Arts, Winston-Salem, North Carolina.*

DON'T TREAD ON ME

3. The yellow banner with the coiled rattlesnake is commonly called the Gadsden Flag. According to the South Carolina Congressional journals, "Col. Gadsden presented to the Congress an elegant standard, such as is to be used by the commander in chief of the American navy; being a yellow field, with a lively representation of a rattlesnake in the middle, in the attitude of going to strike, and these words underneath 'Don't Tread on Me.'"

4. Many prominent citizens were confined in the Provost Dungeon by the British during the Revolution. This photograph is a reenactment by the Old Exchange Players. *Photograph by John W. Clark, courtesy of the Old Exchange and Provost Dungeon.*

5. President George Washington's visit to Charleston was commemorated by this painting. *Portrait by John Trumbull, from the City Hall Collection, Charleston, South Carolina.*

6. The streets of Charles Town were crowded with curious and outraged spectators when the British led Isaac Hayne to the gallows. *Painting by Carroll N. Jones Jr., 1973. Courtesy of the South Carolina Historical Society.*

7. This Wedgwood slave medallion in black on yellow jasper dates to 1787. The image of the slave in chains was adopted by the Abolition Society of England and used extensively by abolitionists in America. *Used by courtesy of the Wedgwood Museum Trust, Staffordshire, England.*

8. "The Arrival of the Mail" was painted by John Blake White in 1837, during the time that the Exchange Building served as the post office in Charleston. *From the City Hall Collection, Charleston, South Carolina.*

THE ILLUSTRATED LONDON NEWS

SLAVE SALE, CHARLESTON, SOUTH CAR

9. (Previous Page) This engraving of a slave auction in Charleston appeared in *Illustrated London News* on November 29, 1856, and was accompanied by the following text:

A SLAVE-AUCTION in South Carolina differs in some respects from a Virginian negro sale. Whilst in the latter case the disposal of human property is made rather a matter of necessity than of boast, and this offensive feature is hidden as much as possible in out-of-the-way places from the view of all but those who purposely visit those unwholesome precincts, in Charleston, South Carolina, on the contrary, matters are in no way minced; and the barter of the blackamoors takes place close to the Exchange, which also subserves the purposes of a post-office. So that when the European traveller wends his way thereto, through dusty and ill-paved streets, it may be in search of a letter from home and for tidings of Old England, he is compelled to witness the severance of those ties which make a home, and to blush for the unworthy descendants who can thus profane the freedom cherished by their British ancestry. To a certain extent the local Mercury *will have prepared him for the spectacle, when he reads such announcements as the following:*

AN ENTIRE GANG OF NEGROES.

Notice. -Particular attention is called to the sale at auction, this day, at eleven o'clock, by Alonzo J. White, of a very prime gang of negroes, who have been accustomed to the culture of rice. Until within the last five years they cultivated sea-island cotton. These negroes are very orderly and well disciplined, and have been organised and worked as a gang. Among them are carpenters and a cooper.

Courtesy of the Avery Research Center for African American History and Culture.

10. "Am I Not a Man and a Brother?" is an example of flyers that were distributed by abolitionist societies. The image of the supplicant slave in chains was taken from the Abolition Society of England. This broadside was sold by the New York Anti-Slavery Society and sold through the mail by abolitionist newspapers. The poem by John Greenleaf Whittier is titled "Our Countrymen in Chains".

11. (Below and opposite) GLC 8551. Abolitionist Tokens. Pair of metal abolitionist tokens, one depicting a male figure with inscription "AM I NOT A MAN AND A BROTHER," and the other depicting a female figure with inscription "AM I NOT A WOMAN AND A SISTER." *The Gilder Lehrman Collection, courtesy of The Gilder Lehrman Institute of American History, New York.*

12. A conjectural view looking east on Broad Street toward the Exchange during the Civil War. *Painting by Mort Kunstler, courtesy of the Old Exchange and Provost Dungeon.*

13. A Civil War-period photograph of the Exchange Building from the Mathew Brady Collection. *Courtesy of the National Archives.*

Mannequins on display in the Provost Dungeon represent patriots held prisoner by the British during the Revolution. *Photograph by Andrew Miller.*

carried in her pockets for him."[28] Young Martha Milner was a heroine in her own right, for "at the age of 14 she received over her eye a bayonet thrust from an accursed Tory Captain as She threw her arms around a Young Brother to protect him."[29]

While a teenaged Martha Milner smuggled rice to her father in the dungeon, other women found themselves within the vaults. Eliza Wilkinson wrote letters describing conditions in Charles Town during the British occupation. She tells of women, as well as men, confined to the Provost.

> *S. Carolina groans under the British yoke; her sons and daughters are exiled, driven from their native land; and their pleasant habitations seized by the insulting victors. "Violence and oppression, and sword law, spread o'er the plains, and refuge none is found." Those who are suffered to remain, are entirely at their mercy; their property is taken and detained from them. When they complain, they are insulted and laughed at; and upon the least suspicion imprisoned, ladies not excepted.*[30]
>
> *I have also had a letter from Capt. ———; he advises me to take care whom I speak to, and not to be very saucy; for the two Miss Sarazens were put in Provost, and very much insulted for some trifle or other. Did you ever hear the like?*[31]

33

Another of those confined in the Provost was Peter Sinkler. A gentleman of stature and influence during the Revolution, Sinkler's location was betrayed to the British by his brother-in-law, James Boisseau. Sinkler was captured in the swamps near his home, Lifeland, and transported to the cellars of the Exchange without having an opportunity to bid his family farewell. Typhus fever soon ended the misery of his confinement, but a handwritten entry in old records suggests that Peter Sinkler's dedication to the American cause was evident in death as well as life. An address dated 1858 mentions Peter Sinkler's story with an added notation: "His body lies under the chancell of St. Phillip's church and he was secretly buried while his casket which was supposed to house his body was filled with ammunition and carried to the army by his request."[32] Surely the heroic Sinkler is worthy of remembrance in the story of the Exchange.

Isaac Hayne was perhaps the most prominent American to be executed for treason against the crown. The son of a pioneer planter, Hayne lived on a prosperous rice plantation called Hayne Hall. He also owned Pear Hill and Sycamore Plantations, several lots in Charles Town and Beaufort, and acreage Upcountry. He served as a colonel of the militia in the Revolutionary army. How Hayne was first captured is open to question, but it is known that he signed an agreement "to act as a British subject as long as the British controlled the area," in order to gain freedom to return to his wife and children, who were lying ill with smallpox. The tide of the war was turning, and Hayne rejoined the militia in territory controlled by the Americans. He was taken prisoner in a surprise attack and confined to the Exchange.

The British then held a court of inquiry, and Hayne was informed of the consequences: "Lord Rawdon and the commandant Lieutenant Colonel Nisbet Balfour have resolved upon his execution." Two forty-eight-hour delays were granted.

The night before Hayne's execution, his three children in Charles Town were allowed to visit their father. They were brought to the Provost by the same aunt who had taken the youngsters to plead on their knees before Balfour for their father's life.

William Edward Hayne was only five years old. His mother and two sisters, one of them his twin, had died of smallpox just a year before. The little boy had been so near death that a coffin was made for his tiny body. When William recovered from the pox he remembered seeing the coffin

Isaac Hayne's children said their farewells on the eve of their father's execution in 1781. *Sketch by Mary A. Anderson.*

that the family had thought would be his. Now, one year later, the child was taken to see his father for the last time. Years later he would write: "My father was confined in the North East Room of the present Custom House then called the Provost—The night previous to his Execution I recollect going there with brother Isaac (then 14) and my Sister Sarah (then 11) in Company with my Aunt Mrs. Peronneau and her daughter…I recollect upon my last visit to my father seeing upon one side of the door of the room of his confinement a Hessian soldier or Centinal on the (other) side a Coffin covered with Black Broad Cloth and lined with white." [33]

How terrifying it must have been for a five-year-old to see his own coffin and, within the same year, that of his father the night before his hanging.

On August 4, 1781, Isaac Hayne was led to the gallows. A contemporary described the hero's last day:

> *The streets were crowded with thousands of anxious spectators…When the city barrier was past, and the instrument of his catastrophe appeared full in view, a faithful friend by his side observed to him, "that he hoped he would exhibit an example of the manner in which an American can die." He answered with the utmost tranquillity, "I will endeavor to do so." He*

ascended the cart with a firm step and serene aspect. He enquired of the executioner, who was making an attempt to get the cap over his eyes, what he wanted? Upon being informed of this design, the colonel replied, "I will only take leave of my friends, and be ready." He then affectionately shook hands with three gentlemen—recommended his children to their care—and gave the signal for the cart to move.[34]

The execution sparked such a protest that its inhumanity was debated throughout the colonies. After the victory at Yorktown, the Continental Congress entertained a motion to take revenge for Hayne's nefarious hanging on their most prominent prisoner, Lord Cornwallis. Ultimately, however, only song, poem and story immortalized the hero's name.[35]

At the end of the Revolutionary War, the British withdrew from Charles Town. The same Daniel Stevens who had been chained in the Provost became sheriff under the new government. The governor ordered all remaining "Strangers and Foreigners," and any citizens who had helped the British, to surrender. Sheriff Stevens arrested "all such and put them in

The Exchange Building was a center of activity on Charleston's waterfront. *Painting by Gil Petroff, courtesy of the old Exchange and Provost Dungeon.*

confinement and confined about 126 persons, who were amenable to the above Law, and they were confined as prisoners in the upper part of the Exchange I had made my Prison"[36] It is a tribute to the character of the man that after spending two months chained in the building's basement, he confined his prisoners on the upper floors. Stevens continued in government service, serving as intendant (mayor) of the city of Charleston in 1819 and 1820.

The Early Federal Period, 1783–1820

With the end of colonial rule, the newly founded states took possession of all "crown" property. The Exchange Building was assigned to the city of Charleston by the government of South Carolina. Ownership was settled on August 13, 1783, in the Act to Incorporate Charleston, and at this time Charles Town became Charleston.

Article V of the law stated, in part, that the "following public lands and buildings within the said city, viz: the lands appropriated for the Exchange, the beef market, the lower market, the fish market, the market at the Western end of Broad Street, with the buildings respectively thereon" were to be vested, fee simple, in the City Council.[37]

It is also clear from this act that the city government was functioning on the top floor of the Exchange. Article IX contains this reference: "an intendant shall be chosen from among the wardens by the inhabitants of all the wards, at the city hall, over the exchange."[38]

Perhaps the choice of words "city hall, over the exchange" should be emphasized. During this period, it is apparent that the open arcade on the first floor served as a place for business and social gatherings, while the second floor, enclosed, served as a city hall for one of America's most important metropolises. The Great Hall was used for many types of assemblages, including local elections; the cellars were once again rented out as warehouse spaces. One official position of incorporated Charleston was the Keeper of the Exchange.

Charleston's Old Exchange Building

With independence, the nation needed a new plan for governing. The first attempt to define the powers and functions of a national government was documented in the Articles of Confederation, but many leaders felt this constitution did not make the central government strong enough to carry out its tasks. Thus a convention was called for and convened in May of 1787 in Philadelphia. The delegates meeting at Independence Hall were to revise the Articles, but their purpose changed. On September 17, 1787, thirty-nine delegates representing twelve states presented a completely new document, which began: "We, the people of the United States, in order to form a more perfect union, establish justice, insure domestic tranquility, provide for the common defense, promote the general welfare, and secure the blessings of liberty to ourselves and our posterity, do ordain and establish this Constitution for the United States of America." Soon copies were carried to every state in the Union.

The plan for ratification was designed to avoid the problems that had held up adoption of the Articles of Confederation for three and a half years. Delegate voters from each state were to call a convention for the specific purpose of ratification of the Constitution. South Carolina assembled her delegates on May 12, 1788, at Charleston; they met in the Exchange Building.

The one hundred men present in city hall on that first day chose Thomas Bee as chairman of the delegates. The next day, officers were selected and motions entertained. According to the *Journals of the Convention of the State of South Carolina Which Ratified the Constitution of the United States*, May 23, 1788, one committee was appointed "to enquire whether a more commodious place than the City Hall could be procured for the sitting of the Convention." On Wednesday, May 14, Doctor David Ramsay reported for the committee, but no action was taken. On Thursday, the consideration of a "more commodious place" was postponed. The convention continued to convene at city hall until May 23. On that day, the motion to "assent to and ratify the Constitution" was voted on. The resolution carried with 149 ayes and 73 noes. South Carolina was the eighth state to ratify the document. The rules required ratification by nine states for the Constitution to become the law of the land. One month later, New Hampshire's ratification accomplished the necessary number. The four remaining states then had a choice; they could ratify or be left outside of the United States of America. Eventually all thirteen states ratified the Constitution.

The strong emotions and political unrest of the American Revolution did not end in 1788. Perhaps the next passionate event in history that found a focus at the Exchange was public opposition to the Jay Treaty, which was signed in London on November 19, 1794. The agreement was secured by diplomat John Jay, who spent a year in London trying to prevent another war between the newly formed United States and Britain. When the terms of the treaty became known in this country, many Americans—Southerners in particular—were furious. Jay was supposed to obtain an agreement that would stop the British from seizing neutral ships; instead, the United States had to give up her definition of neutral shipping for another twelve years.

Another Jay Treaty provision stated that Britain did not have to compensate Americans for slaves kidnapped or freed during the Revolutionary War. According to another section of the treaty, Britain would not stop her navy from halting American vessels and seizing alleged British subjects for forced service as seamen on British warships—a practice known as impressment. Americans did not care if British citizens were forced to serve in the navy, but they were angry because American citizens were being taken off American vessels.

The citizens of Charleston were particularly enraged by the treaty. South Carolina had a slave-based economy, and Charlestonians had lost many slaves when the British evacuated the city. Britain's refusal to reimburse slave owners was a crucial blow to the economy. Moreover, Charleston depended on trade for survival, and those were the days of the great sailing ships; the crops of Carolina were carried to other parts of the country and world largely by sea. Merchants were unhappy with the prospect that ships might be stopped and men seized by the British. There was nothing in the Jay Treaty that favored the local population.

It was under such circumstances that Christopher Gadsden, a leader in the Revolution, addressed Charleston's irate citizens. Gadsden's colorful rhetoric is representative of the passions that prevailed at a public meeting in opposition to the treaty. Gadsden announced within the halls of the Exchange that he would "as soon send a favorite virgin to a Brothel, as a man to England to make a treaty."[39]

Charles Fraser, a Charleston artist and author of the period, remembered a more visual outpouring of public hatred for England. "The excitement was tremendous," he wrote.

> *Among other manifestations of it, was a gallows erected in front of the Exchange, in Broad Street, on which were suspended six effigies, designed to represent the prominent advocates of* [George]

Christopher Gadsden led the Sons of Liberty in South Carolina in 1765. A colonel in the Continental army, he represented South Carolina in the Continental Congress in 1775. *Portrait attributed to Rembrandt Peale, from the City Hall Collection, Charleston, South Carolina.*

Washington's policy, who had maintained the treaty, and whose names are now recorded with honor in the history of our country—John Jay, John Adams, Timothy Pickering, Jacob Read, and William Loughton Smith—who had warmly advocated in the House of Representatives, the appropriation necessary for carrying the treaty into effect. The sixth effigy was his satanic majesty. They remained the whole day, polluted by every mark of indignity, and, in the evening, were carried off to Federal green, where they were burnt.[40]

In spite of similar opposition throughout the United States, the Jay Treaty was ratified by the Senate in 1795.

Despite the restrictions and fears imposed by the Jay Treaty, shipping returned with fervor once the Revolutionary War was over. Since the customs offices were in the Exchange Building, all ships entering and leaving Charleston reported and paid their duties there. The following report of the collector in 1784 gives a very good picture of the activity in Charleston's harbor. The principal export was rice, the major import slaves and the number of recorded vessels exceeded six hundred.

And from the 14th November, 1783 to 3d December, 1784 (being the crop of 1783) the following articles were exported.

Rice,	58,923 barrels.
Do.	6,102 half do.
Indigo,	2,051 Casks.
Tobacco,	2,680 hogsheads.
Deer skins,	651 hhds & bales.
Pitch,	4,877 barrels.
Tar,	2,489 do.
Turpentine,	7,331 do.
Lumber,	705,200 feet.
Shingles,	1,072,000
Staves,	402,100
Indian corn,	14,080 bushels.
Sole leather { hides,	887
sides,	2,703
Hemp,	3 tons.
Flax seed,	171 casks.
Reeds,	147,750

Exported in 90 ships, 10 snows, 148 brigs, 163 sloops, 259 schooners, 1 dogger, and 2 cutters. Measuring 50,961 tons.

Negroes imported in 1783,
From Africa and the West Indies 1,003
From St. Augustine, &c   167—1,170

Negroes imported in 1784,
From Africa and the West Indies, 4,020
From St. Augustine,   1,372—5,392

Total Negroes imported in 1783, and 1784.   6,562

George Abbot Hall, *Collector*[40]

The Great Hall of the Exchange was often used for entertainments. Traveling companies and performers had appeared in Charleston since British actor Anthony Ashton's stay in the city in 1703. Godwin's Company of Comedians occupied the "Hall of the Exchange" until they moved to a new theatre on Inspection Square about 1786.[41]

Dennis Ryan's American Company of Comedians arrived in 1785. The theatre they had planned to use was destroyed in one of the city's many fires, so the performance was held at the Exchange. Converting the hall to a suitable theatre with transparent scenery, the company gave a production typical of early American performances. The newspaper notice read in part:

By Permission
This Evening, March 28th, 1785
The Theatre in the City Exchange
of Charleston
Will be Opened by the American Company
of Comedians
With a Tragedy
Inscribed to his Excellency, General Washington
Called the
ROMAN FATHER[42]

Advocates of the Jay Treaty were hanged in effigy at the Exchange Building. *Sketch by Mary A. Anderson.*

The Roman Father was typical of patriotic and heroic tributes to George Washington that played throughout the new nation. The Ryan company production took place in the Great Hall, where six years later the subject of that adulation would be entertained in the flesh. Since the history of the United States is not complete without the presence of George Washington, it is fitting that Washington came to Charleston, considering the important place the city held in colonial and revolutionary America; it is also appropriate that the father of our country spent time in the Exchange with many of the most prominent personages of America.

The first official census of the United States, taken in 1790, demonstrates Charleston's importance. It records the great cities of the newborn nation: New York, with a population of 32,328; Philadelphia, with 28,522; Boston, with 18,320; and running a close fourth, Charleston, with 16,359. The total population of the United States according to the 1790 census was 3,893,635.

George Washington arrived in Charleston on Monday, May 2, 1791, and stayed almost a week. The Exchange Building, as the center of official and social activities, saw his presence often. On the first day of his visit, the president was conducted to the Exchange to watch a procession of dignitaries. On Tuesday he was treated to a public dinner given at the Exchange.[43] The following day Washington was entertained at a very elegant "dancing Assembly at the Exchange at which were 256 elegantly dressed and handsome ladies."[44] Those words are Washington's. A more vivid account of the occasion appeared in Charleston's newspaper the next day:

> *In the evening a splendid ball was given by the city corporation, which the President of the United States honored with his presence. There was a numerous and brilliant assemblage of ladies and a great number of gentlemen present. The ladies were all superbly dressed, and most of them wore ribbons with different inscription, expressive of their respect and esteem for the President, such as "long live the President," &c, &c. Joy, satisfaction and gratitude illuminated every countenance and revelled in each heart, whilst the demonstrations of grateful respect shewn him seemed to give him the most heartfelt satisfaction, which…displayed itself in his countenance.*
>
> *The beautiful arch of lamps in front of the Exchange was illuminated; and over the entrance there was a superb transparency, in the centre "Deliciis Patriae."* [For the delight of the Country] *and at the top "G. W."*
>
> *The fusilear company was drawn up before the Exchange to maintain order, and exhibited a very pleasing appearance. In short every circumstance of the evening's entertainment was truly picturesque of the most splendid elegance.*[45]

On the evening of the concert in Washington's honor, the Great Hall is described as beautifully decorated. "On this occasion [it] had received considerable alteration, and was decorated with various ornaments—the pillars were ingeniously entwined with laurel, and the following devices inscribed in different parts of the Hall: 'With grateful praises of the hero's fame, We'll teach our infant's tongues to lisp his name.'"[46] The celebration was a fitting tribute from one of the wealthiest cities in the young nation to its first president.

George Washington spoke admirably of the ladies of Charleston during his visit in 1791 when he was entertained at the Exchange. *Sketch by Mary A. Anderson.*

Apparently, President Washington was quite impressed by Charleston's ladies during his visit, for he comments on them often in his diary. Washington's words again, dated Thursday, May 5: "In the evening went to a Concert at the Exchange at wch. there were at least 400 ladies in the number and appearance of wch. exceeded any thing of the kind I had ever seen."[47]

One Charleston resident, Charles Fraser, recalled Washington's visit as "that imposing occasion, the most prominent is of the person of the great man, as he stood upon the steps of the Exchange, uncovered, amidst the enthusiastic acclamations of the citizens."[48] Of the concert and ball given in the hall of the Exchange, Fraser remembered, "On that occasion, the ladies wore fillets, or bandeaus (I have one of the bandeaus worn on that occasion.) of white riband, interwoven in their head-dress, with the head of Washington painted on them, and the words, 'Long live the President,' in gilt letters. Every hand that could hold a pencil, professional or amateur, was enlisted to furnish them."[49]

In 1809, Richard Harbowski put together a city directory for Charleston. His list of "Public Buildings and Societies" includes the Exchange. The entry illustrates the variety of activities, civil and commercial, which continued in the structure: "Exchange, east end of Broad Street, in which are kept the Offices of Clerk of Council, City Treasurer, City Sheriff, Clerk of Inferior City Court, City Enquirer and Assessor, Harbor Master, City Marshall and Messenger of Council, and Keeper of the Exchange."[50]

Abraham Botte's *Charleston Directory and Stranger's Guide* was published in 1816. He lists six offices on the first and second floors of the Exchange. The entry, "city hall, second floor of exchange,"[51] shows that city government continued at this building until the move to Charleston's present city hall at Meeting and Broad Streets in 1818. On February 14, 1818, the city of Charleston sold the Exchange Building to the federal government for $60,000.[52]

In the spring of 1819, President James Monroe made a state visit to Charleston. The *Charleston Courier* reported on Friday, April 30, that: "Yesterday morning the President, in company with the Secretary of War, and Major Gen. Thomas Pinckney visited the Custom-House. Thence they proceeded, in company with the Governor of the State…in the steam boat *Charleston*, accompanied by a Band of Music, to visit the Forts in the harbor."

President Monroe would have observed the many activities that continued at the Exchange. Although city government moved, the building continued to serve as Charleston's post office, the custom house, a meeting hall and a witness to the trading of slaves.

The Nineteenth Century, 1818–1896

For most of the nineteenth century the United States used the Exchange as a post office and customhouse. Considering the thriving port city and the significance of the mail as a source of communication at that time, life at the building was no less exciting than in previous decades. The mail was what linked America to the rest of the world, and letters were tremendously important. In support of this premise, one foreign traveler's interest in the mail resulted in a superb description of the activity surrounding the Exchange Building, both as a post office and as a central location for community commerce. One day in 1829, Captain Basil Hall, an officer of the Royal Navy, wrote:

> But after all, the most picturesque object in every traveller's landscape is generally the Post-office; and drawing myself away from these delicious scenes, some real and some imaginary, I set off in quest of letters. My attention, however, was arrested on the way by a circumstance which I might certainly have expected in Charleston, but somehow had not looked for. On reaching the Exchange, in the centre of which the Post-office is placed, I heard the sound of several voices in the street, like those of an auctioneer urging an audience to bid for his goods. I walked to the side of the gallery overlooking a court or square, in which a number of people were collected to purchase slaves and other property. One man was selling a horse

on which he was mounted, and riding up and down the streets; another, in the same way, was driving about in a curricle, bawling out to the spectators to make an offer for his carriage and horses. But of course my attention was most taken up with the slave market.

A long table was placed in the middle of the street, upon which the negroes were exposed, not one by one, but in families at a time. From this conspicuous station they were shown off by two auctioneers, one at each end of the table, who called out the biddings, and egged on the purchasers by chanting the praises of their bargains.

These parties of slaves varied in number. The first consisted of an old, infirm woman, a stout broad-shouldered man, apparently her son, his wife, and two children. The auctioneer, having told the names of each, and described their qualifications, requested the surrounding gentlemen to bid. One hundred dollars for each member of the family, or 500 for the whole party, was the first offer. This gradually rose to 150, at which sum they were finally knocked down; that is to say, 750 dollars for the whole, or about £170. Several other families were then put up in succession, who brought from 250 to 260 dollars each member, including children at the breast, as well as old people quite incapable of work.

The next party was exceedingly interesting. The principal person was a stout well-built man, or, as the auctioneer called him, "a fellow, who was a capital driver."[53] His wife stood by his side—a tall, finely proportioned, and really handsome woman, though as black as jet. Her left arm encircled a child about six months old, who rested, in the Oriental fashion, on the hip bone. To preserve the balance, her body was inclined to the right, where two little urchins clung to her knee, one of whom, evidently much frightened, clasped its mother's hand, and never relinquished it during the sale which followed. The husband looked grave and somewhat sad; but there was a manliness in the expression of his countenance, which appeared strange in a person placed in so degraded a situation. What struck me most, however, was an occasional touch of anxiety about his eye as it glanced from bidder to bidder, when new offers were made. It seemed to imply a perfect acquaintance with the character of the different parties competing for him—and his happiness or misery for life, he might think, turned upon a word!

The whole of this pretty group were neatly dressed, and altogether so decorous in their manner, that I felt my interest in them rising at every instant. The two little boys, who appeared to be twins, kept their eyes fixed steadily on their mother's face. At first they were quite terrified, but eventually they became as tranquil as their parents. The struggle amongst the buyers continued for nearly a quarter of an hour, till at length they were knocked down for 290 dollars a-piece, or 1450 dollars for the whole family, about £330 Sterling.

I learnt from a gentleman afterwards that the negroes, independently of the important consideration of being purchased by good masters, have a singular species of pride on these occasions in fetching a high price; holding it, amongst themselves, as disgraceful to be sold for a small sum of money. This fact, besides showing how difficult it is to subdue utterly the love of distinction, may perhaps be useful in teaching us never to take for granted that any one boasting the human form, however degraded in the scale, is without some traces of generous feeling.[54]

After observing the slave auction, Captain Hall proceeded to check for his mail inside the Exchange. Just how did the all-important postal service work in this period before the Civil War?

Mail from the interior regions arrived in Charleston by stagecoach. Some cities were served only once a week, so one can imagine the excitement when the stagecoach arrived at the Exchange to drop off its bag of letters.

Door-to-door delivery was a thing of the future; every person and representatives from every business had to go to the post office to pay the appropriate fee and claim their mail. The building served as a gathering place for those awaiting correspondence carried on arriving stages and ships. The post carried by sea came from port cities such as New York and Philadelphia, as well as from foreign countries. When regular shipping was interrupted by the Civil War, blockade runners risked their lives to carry supplies and mail past the Northern blockade. No matter how the mail arrived—whether by stagecoach, under a flag of truce, on the train or surreptitiously through Union lines—the excitement among local citizens was great.

During the years when the Exchange Building served as Charleston's only post office, many changes took place in the life of a letter. The first gummed stamps were issued in 1847. Before that, a postmark showed the date and city of origin. The mark was made by a die of either metal or carved wood, dipped in ink and stamped on the letter. Such marks were called handstamps.[55]

These handstamps were used in the Charleston post office. *Courtesy of the South Carolina Historical Society.*

Postal charges were determined by the number of sheets of paper to be mailed. Each sheet counted as a letter. Since envelopes added an extra sheet and therefore an extra charge, most letters were not in envelopes. People wrote on a single page, folded it, and sealed the correspondence with a blob of hard wax, known as sealing wax. If the wax seal was broken, the person who received the letter could tell if it had been opened.

For the first half of the nineteenth century, letters could be sent "collect," meaning the person who picked up the mail paid the postage. Unclaimed letters contributed no fees to government coffers. Since some mail carried no street or box address, there were often a lot of unclaimed letters. The postmaster would place advertisements in the newspaper listing unclaimed letters; according to these notices, unclaimed mail was available to anyone willing to pay for the advertisement and the postage due on the letter. In 1855, the system was modified and prepayment of postage was required in Charleston.[56]

Coin scarcities also presented problems. Change in small denominations was hard to come by, so postal patrons were allowed to redeem letters with foreign coins. The coin shortage was so widespread that charge accounts were often arranged, and citizens were billed for mail service on a monthly basis.[57]

Perhaps the best understanding of the postal service before the Civil War comes from public documents of the time. The *Charleston City Directory* of 1829 printed the following postal information:

Thomas W. Bacot, Post-Master
Mail Arrangement

Northern-Due every day at 3 p.m. Closes every day at 7 o'clock p.m. Mails are made up for Cheraw, Chesterfield, Darlington, Marr's Bluff, Society Hill and Springville every Tuesday, Thursday, and Sunday, and are due from those offices on Tuesday, Thursday and Saturday.

Southern-Due every day at 5 o'clock p.m. Closes every day at 7 ½ o'clock p.m. By this route the following mails are due every Thursday viz from St. Augustine, Jacksonville, St. Mary's, Frederica, Ratcliffe, Tuckersville, and Brunswick, Georgia, and are dispatched from this office every Monday.

A Mail is due from Beaufort every Tuesday, Thursday and Saturday and one is made up for that place on the same evenings.

Due from Augusta every Sunday, Wednesday, and Friday at half past 6 p.m. Columbia: Due on Monday, Thursday and Saturday at 3 p.m.

Rates of Postage

Rates-For single letters composed of one piece of paper, carried any distance not exceeding 30 miles, 6 cents; over 30 miles and not exceeding 400, 18 ½ cents; over 400, 25 cents. Double letters or those composed of two pieces of paper and double the above rates. Triple letters with triple the amount.

The notice also included postage rates for newspapers, magazines and ship letters. A special note added, "No Books can be sent by post." Business hours were also stated: "The office is open every day except Sunday, from 8 a.m. in the winter and 7 a.m. in the summer, until 8 p.m. except for half past 2 to half past 3 p.m. and during the openings and assorting of the Northern and Southern mails. On Sunday the office will be opened from 9 to 10 o'clock a.m."

In 1835, a dramatic incident occurred at the post office. By this time, slavery had become a widely argued issue that stirred passions throughout the United States. Congressmen in Washington repeatedly debated and compromised, trying to maintain a balance between slave-holding regions and free lands, but emotions on the subject were extreme. Anti-slavery organizations in the North became dedicated to abolition, the end of slavery everywhere. In 1833 the British abolitionists won freedom for slaves in the West Indies. This fired up American reformers, and Northern

This engraving of the Exchange was published for the *Philadelphia Album* in 1828. The building was serving as the post office for Charleston at that time. *Courtesy of the Old Exchange and Provost Dungeon.*

abolitionists began bombarding the South with literature. The practice infuriated Charlestonians. A contemporary local newspaper account described the situation:

> *We published a few days since, a notice of the proceedings of the Anti-Slavery Society of New York, threatening to inundate the Southern States with the incendiary publications. That threat they have now fulfilled. By the steam boat which arrived here yesterday from New York thousands of copies of these infamous publications, consisting of newspapers and pamphlets, filled with the most scandalous and seditious matter and illustrated by suitable prints were received at the Post Office, addressed to a number of respectable gentlemen here and among them, we believe, the clergy of all denominations. We give this information in order to put our southern friends on their guard.*[58]

The paper goes on to recommend that the copies be returned to the publisher.

Many local citizens decided to handle the matter by destroying the mailed publications. "Such was the excitement in our city caused by the arrival of the incendiary pamphlets and papers which almost monopolized the U.S. mail on Wednesday that a crowd of two or three hundred citizens assembled that night for the purpose of seizing and destroying them. These citizens were met by Lieut. Brown of the City Guard near the Exchange and persuaded to disperse."[59]

Alfred Huger was postmaster at the time. It was his duty to protect the mail and see that it was delivered to Charleston's citizens. He began communications between local leaders and authorities in Washington to find a solution to the problem. Then another band of citizens took the situation in hand. The local newspaper described the event: "Between the hours of 10 and 11 o'clock that night [Wednesday, July 29] a number of persons assembled about the Exchange and, without any noise or disturbance, but on the contrary, with coolness and deliberation, made a forcible entry into the post office by wrenching open one of its windows and carried off the packages containing the incendiary matter."[60] The papers were destroyed in a public bonfire on the parade ground in front of The Citadel.[61]

Alfred Huger was unable to carry out his responsibility for delivering the mail. Incensed, "Post Master Huger got ready his shot gun to die, if necessary, before he would permit such another outrage."[62] Huger was not

Alfred Huger, Charleston postmaster from 1835 until 1865. *From the City Hall Collection, Charleston, South Carolina.*

the only person angered. By destroying United States mail, Charlestonians helped publicize the abolitionist cause in the nation. Anti-slavery societies won sympathy as a minority, and were seen as being denied the right to send their ideas through the mail. Abolitionist feelings continued to grow, and by 1861 the Northern states were morally armed for that most terrible conflict, the Civil War.

Alfred Huger maintained his position as postmaster from December 19, 1834, until 1865, and was charged with the duty to protect and deliver the mail throughout the Civil War. When South Carolina joined the Confederate States of America, Huger remained in his position as an agent of the Confederacy. One of his duties was to have postage stamps printed by Evans and Cogswell, a firm located across the street from the Exchange, later to become the Walker, Evans and Cogswell Company.

Union cannonades during the war took their toll on the old Exchange. Not wanting to endanger lives, city officials removed the post office from the Exchange on August 26, 1863.[63] It functioned at various locations in the city for the remainder of the war.

After the war, the Exchange was in a dilapidated state. Questions arose as to whether the structure should be repaired or torn down to make way for

This engraving showing a view of Broad Street in the first year of the Civil War appeared in *Harper's Weekly*, December 28, 1861. Note the Exchange Building with the Palmetto Flag flying from its cupola. *Courtesy of the Old Exchange and Provost Dungeon.*

a new post office. The federal government, as the building's owner, had the responsibility of deciding, though local citizens voiced their own opinions. Pride in the Exchange's history prompted many people to call for the old building's repair and continued use.

On July 2, 1870, the local newspaper reported the Old Exchange would be repaired. The work was done under federal architects J.R. Willet and T.H. Oakshott and Charleston building contractor and architect Christopher Trumbo.[64] Once the building was restored, the post office again operated in the Exchange and remained there until Charleston's new post office at the corner of Broad and Meeting Streets was completed in 1896.

During its post office period, the Exchange also served as a customhouse on the second floor. The Exchange Building continued to be Charleston's center of commerce as well as the center of communications for most of the nineteenth century.

During the early years of our government, income from customs was the mainstay of the treasury. Thus, whatever the state of protective sentiment, the revenue motive was always present. In the two years 1789 and 1790, customs and tonnage duties—mainly customs—contributed approximately 88 percent of the total ordinary receipts of the federal government. As an annual average, from 1801 to 1810 the same sources provided about 92 percent. In the decade from 1811 to 1820, due to the use of internal revenues during the War of 1812, the amount declined to 77 percent, but rose again to the previous level in most of the years prior to 1860. In fact, as an annual average for the decade ending in 1860, customs and tonnage duties contributed about 90 percent of total ordinary receipts. The use of certain excises after the Civil War somewhat reduced the importance of customs, but this source still remained as one of the most important general divisions of income until the introduction of more varied domestic taxes after 1915.

Prior to the Civil War, Congress passed six major tariff acts. The preamble of the law of 1789, the first of its kind in our history, indicated that the purpose was to "support the government," to "discharge the debts of the United States" and to promote the "encouragement and protection of manufactures." Duties were imposed on a rather long list of commodities. Some were purely revenue items, such as coffee, cocoa, tea and sugar; others combined the purpose of revenue and protection.[65] One can imagine the importance of the customs office in one of America's major ports.

In 1879, the U.S. Customs Service in Charleston moved to a new building at 200 East Bay Street, a grand Greek Revival building where it still operates today.

After 1896, all federal offices had vacated the Exchange Building, and it stood empty in its prominent position looking down Broad Street. What was to become of the pre-revolutionary structure?

Patriotism Prevails in the Twentieth Century, 1896 and After

The United States government decided by act of Congress to sell the Exchange Building in the late 1890s, but the act was not executed immediately. In 1898, the building was turned over to the United States Light House Service. Meanwhile, the act had sounded the alarm for a group of women who feared what the future might hold for this building that had been witness to history since 1771. The Rebecca Motte Chapter of the Daughters of the American Revolution (DAR), whose foresight and interest in the preservation of the Exchange determined, at the first talk of selling the building, that they would save it.[66]

When the sale was finally ordered in 1912, these women met the occasion with the concern and perseverance that marked their association with the Exchange Building for the rest of its history. Alarmed by rumors that a builder was interested in the site, the Rebecca Motte Chapter took action.[67] A committee's efforts were rewarded on March 4, 1913, when a bill passed by Congress authorized the secretary of the treasury "to convey, by quitclaim deed, the Old Exchange…to the Order of Daughters of the American Revolution in and of the State of South Carolina, to be held by it as a historical memorial in trust for such use, care, and occupation thereof by the Rebecca Motte Chapter of said order…as the said chapter shall in its judgment deem to best subserve the preservation of said colonial building and promote the honorable and patriotic purpose for which the grant is requested."[68] The deed provided for the Light House Service to continue use of the building until provisions could be made for other quarters.

Although they had owned the building since 1917, the members of the Rebecca Motte Chapter did not hold their first meeting in the Exchange until March 9, 1921. With the approach of World War I, the Chapter decided a "patriotic purpose" would be served by placing the Exchange at the disposal of the War Department. The building became the headquarters for General Leonard Wood during World War I, and the Light House Service continued its residency. It wasn't until March 1933 that a newspaper article stated that the Sixth Light House District would move in a few months from the Exchange to new quarters.[69]

The old walls of the Exchange were to remain in the line of duty, and World War II brought more patriotic scenes to the building. The Charleston *News and Courier* reported on December 31, 1942: "Administration offices of the Coastal Pickets, U.S. Coast Guard, Sixth Naval District moved into the

The Exchange Building was used by the Light House Service. Notice the clock in the pediment. *Courtesy of the Old Exchange and Provost Dungeon.*

[Exchange] building yesterday." The same newspaper article reported that offices of the Huguenot Society were located in the building.

During World War II, even the cellars of the Exchange were called into use. The vaults, which had held tea, gunpowder and chained patriots, now concealed a hidden treasure. In 1947, curious occupants of the building, mostly coast guard personnel, watched "as workmen broke through the brickseal in the dungeon wall and lowered a ladder into the 20-foot-deep vault. With the aid of flashlights, lines were secured to the galvanized wash tubs in which the silver was stored and the tubs were hauled up."

The treasure hoisted into view consisted of sixty-six items known as the Battleship Silver. The silver service had been commissioned by the state of South Carolina and presented to the battleship *South Carolina* on April 11, 1910. These magnificent pieces were handmade with appropriate Caroliniana designs. The punchbowl, with a capacity of seven gallons, is chased with a reproduction of the battleship. Dolphins form the handles and magnolias are the main decoration, with portrait medallions of John Rutledge and John C. Calhoun in relief. On the reverse side is shown "Jasper Planting the Flag" and medallions of Colonel Pierce Butler and General Wade Hampton.

The service had been placed in the custody of the South Carolina Daughters of the American Revolution when the battleship *South Carolina* was scrapped in 1921. The silver was displayed in the Old Exchange until the onset of World War II, when the custodians of the treasure decided to brick the pieces up in the dungeons for safekeeping. For almost six years the valuables had lain hidden, their whereabouts known only to a few members of the DAR. Upon removal in 1947, the Battleship Silver was sent to Columbia for display in the governor's mansion, where it can be seen today.[70]

Preservation and Restoration
in the Twentieth Century

Owning one of the most significant buildings in American history since 1917 has been an awesome responsibility for the Rebecca Motte Chapter of the DAR. Their charge was to maintain the Exchange as a historical monument; their goal became to restore the building to its original splendor. The task required vast amounts of money, but these dedicated women were determined to succeed.

The Chapter worked during the early years of its ownership to save the edifice from decay. The members held rummage sales to raise funds while providing goods to local citizens at reasonable prices. They also held bake sales and card parties.[71]

One example of their concerted efforts can be found in an article from the Charleston *Evening Post* in 1924. "The Rebecca Motte Chapter, Daughters of the American Revolution…replaced the roof, [and] restored the iron work at the top of the steps where George Washington once stood to review troops marching along Broad Street. Their latest project has been the decoration of the Chapter room to some semblance of its former Glory."[72] The diligent work went on for years.

It was during this period that space in the building was rented to a fencing school, and thus the clash of arms sounded once more within the walls. This activity helped raise needed funds for restoration. Perhaps the first tangible effort at restoration of the Exchange Building and the creation of the

This portion of the original sea wall was exposed in 1965 during the restoration of the Provost Dungeon. *Photograph by Andrew Simons Jr.*

living museum that it is today came in 1965. Charlestonian C. Harrington Bissell's interest in the Provost resulted in a lease from the Rebecca Motte Chapter. With Thomas E. Thornhill, Bissell took on the ambitious project of returning the cellars to their colonial condition. He wanted to illustrate the outstanding role South Carolina played in world trade and government during the colonial period and the American Revolution.

Upon entering the basement, Bissell found various items of junk, an old furnace, a cistern and much debris. No one was sure what lay beneath the centuries of accumulation. After the initial clean up, a twentieth-century wooden floor was removed in hopes of finding some original flooring. When two more levels were removed, the original underlying brick was discovered.

Revealing this floor brought a new unknown to light: The brickwork covered a large, mysterious mound. Bissell was curious, yet careful, and called for professional help. E. Milby Burton, then director of the Charleston Museum, guided the research efforts, and John Miller, an expert digger, was employed.[73]

When the mysterious mound was finally excavated, the puzzling hump turned out to be a portion of the Half-Moon Battery. Buried for almost two

This skull was found during the 1965 excavation and restoration of the Provost Dungeon. *Courtesy of the Old Exchange and Provost Dungeon.*

centuries, the original wall of Charles Town stood exposed. The digging also yielded many artifacts that demonstrated the commercial importance this city was known to have had in pre-Revolutionary times.[74]

A not-so-common find during the excavation were portions of a human skeleton. The bones were studied by Ted A. Rathbun, a forensic physical anthropologist. He reported, in part, "The human skeletal remains recovered from the Exchange Building represents a young adult male of probably Indian ancestry. At the time of his death, probably 1710–1800 A.D., he suffered from anemia, gum resorption, and in earlier life had a head wound and three episodes of illness or deficient diet."[75] Rathbun estimated the age at death to be twenty to thirty years.

This was a new mystery for the ancient site, a mystery whose solution lies buried somewhere in the past, and a mystery that links the native inhabitants of the area, Indians, to the Exchange story.

Harrington Bissell's objective was to bring history to life—to recreate the experience of patriots held prisoner within the dank basement of the Exchange. Painstaking research was carried out in composing displays for the Provost Dungeon Museum. Local authority Emmett Robinson designed the scenes with accuracy and authenticity, and each life-size model represented a specific individual who was confined in the basement.

Bissell opened the Provost Museum in 1966. He subsequently received various awards for his efforts to reproduce American history in the cellars of the Exchange. With the creation of the Old Exchange Commission and total restoration of the building, Bissell relinquished his role.[76]

As the nation's bicentennial approached, the Rebecca Motte Chapter of the DAR worked with city and state commissions to produce a comprehensive plan for complete restoration of the Exchange and acquisition of funds for the project. Many details had to be decided, and matters could not be resolved in time for the bicentennial celebration, though talks continued. With the help of Governor James B. Edwards, agreements were reached between the Rebecca Motte Chapter and the state Bicentennial Commission. The agreement was presented to the state General Assembly in 1976.

The Old Exchange Commission, established by an act of the General Assembly, was given operative and administrative control of matters relating to the Exchange Building.[77] A lease was signed in December 1976, giving the Old Exchange Commission effective control over most of the building for the next twenty-five years. The commission also had the option to continue control for three more successive twenty-five-year periods.[78]

The first task of the organization was restoration of the entire building. Funding for the work was provided as follows:

State of South Carolina General Fund	*$750,000*
State of South Carolina Bond Proceeds	*360,000*
Economic Development Administration	*400,000*
Coastal Plains Regional Commission	*200,000*
American Revolution Bicentennial Administration	*100,000*
U.S. Department of the Interior	*100,000*
Total	*$1,910,000*

A contract for restoration was executed on August 10, 1979, in the Old Exchange Building. The architectural firm of Simons, Mitchell, Small and Donahue was hired to draw up restoration plans. A low bid of $1,637,000, submitted by Charleston Constructors, Inc., was accepted for the work.[79]

During the complete renovation of the building, John M. Mitchell Jr., who acted as project architect, made some interesting discoveries. The vaulted ceilings of the cellar are only one-brick thick at the point of the vault, an engineering masterpiece. The vaults are leveled above with loads of sand to support the original purbeck stone of the main floor. In the sand, Mitchell found single unbroken oyster shells. It appears that workmen over two hundred years ago helped themselves to oysters growing along the riverbanks at the front of the building, ate the oysters for lunch, then tossed the shells into the sand they were using for fill.

Another discovery was the original wood in the attic of the building. Here huge beams bear the ax marks of hand-hewn timber, and some attic supports are tied together with wedge-shaped bars pounded into metal

The third cupola was added during the restoration. It was finished in time for the opening ceremonies on October 6, 1981. *Courtesy of the Old Exchange and Provost Dungeon.*

bands, another early construction technique. Wooden beams supporting the original cupola were left amid the rafters, and some original window boxes were also discovered. Most window boxes, specifically the part that houses the weights that enable the windows to open and close, are made with several pieces of wood. Those in the Exchange Building were made of a single piece of wood, with the weight chamber hollowed out in dug-out canoe fashion. These are stored in the attic for further study. In addition to window boxes and timbers, capital portions of the eastern pilasters and original interior plaster bound with horsehair are visible in the attic, where they can be studied by scholars.

On the main floor, a closet door opens to reveal an original arch filled with poor-quality "salmon" brick. Within the same closet can be found a unique stucco coating. The finish is beautifully smooth and polished, hand-spattered with various colored paints to resemble granite. The fine stucco coating predates the enclosing of the arches and is one of the earliest finishes applied to the great Exchange.[80]

A workman positions an interior arch during the restoration. *Courtesy of the Old Exchange and Provost Dungeon.*

The Exchange Building viewed from Broad Street during the construction of the third cupola in 1980. *Courtesy of the Old Exchange and Provost Dungeon.*

The Old Exchange and Provost Dungeon was formally opened on October 5, 1981.[81] On August 31, 1989, the City of Charleston assumed the management of the building operations and the personnel. Now, at long last, the Exchange has been restored to its former splendor. Ready to tell the fascinating tale, this witness to American history stands proudly at the foot of Broad Street. The Provost, still dank and without sunlight, speaks of pirates and patriots in chains, of troublesome tea and hidden gunpowder. The arcade level bears the same purbeck stone floor on which strode thousands of merchants, slaves and citizens—the famous and the infamous. The second story holds the Great Hall in which so many figures, from the boisterous patriots of the Revolution to elegant dancers at the ball sponsored for President Washington, played their part in America's story.

Every effort was made to preserve original portions of the building while adapting it to modern usage. The Old Exchange Commission, the City of Charleston, the South Carolina State Society of the Daughters of the American Revolution, and the Rebecca Motte Chapter of the DAR invite visitors to step back into history and visit the Old Exchange, a National Historic Landmark, beautifully restored and open as a living museum.

Architecture

Architecturally, Charleston's Exchange is singular; this structure is the finest example of an English tradition—the exchange-town hall—built in America.

"Exchange" may seem an unusual term today, but two hundred years ago the exchange-town hall was tremendously important. The concept was initiated in England by Sir Thomas Gresham with the erection of the Old Royal Exchange between 1566 and 1571 in London. The multi-purpose plan for this building included an open arcade for use as a trading floor, which supported enclosed upper stories to be used as office space. The style spread throughout England and from there to the American colonies.

The earliest colonial exchange was built in Philadelphia in 1707. There, simple brick arches on the exchange floor supported a meeting hall and above that a roof which was distinguished by a cupola. Another famous example is Boston's Faneuil Hall, a market arcade beneath meeting rooms, built in 1740. Neither building, though, approached the fine ornamentation and dignified scale of their English antecedents. Newport's Brick Market displayed more substance but still lacked grandeur and extensive ornament. It is Charleston's Exchange, completed in 1771, which demonstrates the dignity and decoration appropriate to the English genre.[82]

Charleston's Old Exchange Building

The success of the Charleston building requires some understanding of the style in which it found fulfillment. Best described as American Georgian, the design derives from the monumental buildings of England, where the classic tradition of Palladian architecture combined with the English tradition of Sir Christopher Wren. In reading the words of these two great architects, one sees the derivation of the fine Exchange Building in Charleston.[83]

Andrea Palladio was a sixteenth-century Italian architect who emphasized the symmetry and balance of classical architecture. For most of his life, Palladio built city or country homes for wealthy citizens. One of his most famous buildings, the Villa Rotunda near Vicenze, Italy, has influenced architects for centuries. Palladio wrote:

> *Three things…are chiefly to be considered, without which a building cannot be of any value. These are Convenience, Solidity, and Beauty. For no Edifice can be allowed to be perfect, if it be commodious and not durable; or, if being durable, it be subject to many inconveniences; or if having both solidity and convenience, it has no beauty nor conformity.*
>
> *An edifice may be reckon'd Commodious, when every part of it has its proper place and situation, in respect to its dignity and uses. The Solidity of an Edifice depends upon the care of erecting the walls very plum, and thicker below than above, with good and stout Foundations. As for the beauty of an Edifice, it consists in an exact Proportion of the parts within themselves, and of each part with the whole; for a fine Building ought to appear as an entire and perfect body.*[84]

To Palladio's evaluation of a building, we add the voice of Sir Christopher Wren, perhaps the best-known English architect of the seventeenth century. Wren was called upon to design many buildings, including more than fifty churches, after the great fire that almost leveled London in 1666. His most famous structure is St. Paul's Cathedral in London.

This architect, whose work had a great influence on the buildings of colonial America, wrote as follows:

> *Architecture has its political use; publick Buildings being the Ornament of a country; it establishes a Nation, draws People and Commerce; makes the people love their native Country, which Passion is the Original of all great actions in a Commonwealth.*[85]

Of the exchanges built in America, Charleston's comes the nearest to meeting the requirements of its tradition. For convenience, there was no better location. Built to face the busy harbor, a commercial center, the Exchange stood solid and proud on Charleston's skyline. There is no doubt that the beautification of its east side, by which ships approached, was designed to impress. The façade wore six pilasters and four engaged columns, ten stone urns upon the pediment, and a wreathed oculus, a circular opening. The west side, which looked down Broad Street, had only four flat pilasters, four urns, and a plain oculus.[86]

Experience Charleston's lively harbor two hundred years ago with the new Exchange as its focal point. Josiah Quincy Jr., a New England traveler, in his diary entry on February 28, 1773, wrote:

> We now were off Charlestown Bar, and the wind being right in our teeth we were the whole day beating up. Just before sunset we passed the fort. Charlestown appeared situated between two large spacious rivers, (the one on the right called Cooper River and the other on the left, Ashley River) which here empty themselves into the sea. The number of shipping far surpassed all I had ever seen in Boston. I was told there were then not so many as common at this season, tho' about 350 sail lay off the town. The town struck me very agreeably; but the New Exchange which fronted the place of my landing made a most noble appearance.[87]

If Quincy's diary had continued with a close-up of the Exchange, he would have described the mercantile center of this busy harbor. The merchants conducted their business on the open arcade level, shouting orders to messengers who stood at the beck and call of businessmen. Every ship that entered the harbor was required to send a representative to report to the customs offices and pay required duties. Virtually no major business could be conducted in the city without transactions taking place in the Exchange Building.

The "most noble appearance" that greeted Quincy was certainly no accident. From the very beginning, the Charleston Exchange was meant to be the finest that could be built in America. There is much information available concerning its construction; the original drawings by William Rigby Naylor, and the builder's contract with John and Peter Horlbeck are both extant. Yet questions arise.

William Rigby Naylor was working in Charleston on December 10, 1766, when he signed the plans for the Exchange. These plans come to life rather vividly in a 1774 engraving by Thomas Leitch[88] and a drawing by W.G. Mason in 1780.[89] It appears that Naylor designed the Exchange; the pieces fit, including Naylor's death notice in which he is described as "Architect and Surveyor."[90]

But Naylor's name is not the only one associated with Exchange designs. Thomas Woodin is also referred to in the Statutes at Large for the State of South Carolina.[91] On April 3, 1767, Woodin was granted pay for his drawing and elevation for the intended Exchange. On May 25, 1767: "Charges to be paid…36.15 [36 pounds, 15 shilling current money] to Thomas Woodin for a plan of the intended Exchange." Both Woodin and Naylor are known to have been "teachers of drawing."[92]

Respected historian Gene Waddell resolves the question as follows:

> *William Rigby Naylor signed his name to drawings of the Exchange and added "Invt. et. Delt.," meaning Invenit et Delineavit (He designed and he drew), and thus claimed explicitly to have both designed the building and to have drawn the plans. Since the building follows these plans closely, he deserves to be considered the architect. Naylor advertised to teach architectural drawing specifically. Thomas Woodin may have taught draftsmanship, but his advertisement does not say so; instead, Woodin called himself a "Carver and Cabinet Maker, (who) teaches drawing in all its Branches" (possibly not including architecture at all). Woodin deserves some credit for the Exchange or he would not have been paid so large an amount for a plan, but this probably did not include elevations or floor plans. Instead his plan must have been for what he excelled at most, for carving. He is most likely to have made drawings for the interior woodwork, a practice mentioned in a 1769 advertisement by Ezra Waite. Woodin may well have designed decorations to be carved for the interior (cornices, mantels, etc.), but with the available evidence he cannot be said to have contributed to the overall architectural design that was adopted.[93]*

The contract with the Horlbecks, brothers and partners in business, was signed on December 1, 1767. They were promised 41,740 pounds to construct the building, following detailed specifications and using the finest materials. A few excerpts from the contract give an idea of its content:

> *And the Wall of the East Side to be Six Bricks lengthways thick from the Foundation to the Piazza Floor, the Cellars to be divided into Six apartments and Paved with good Brick on Edge…Two Piers which supports the*

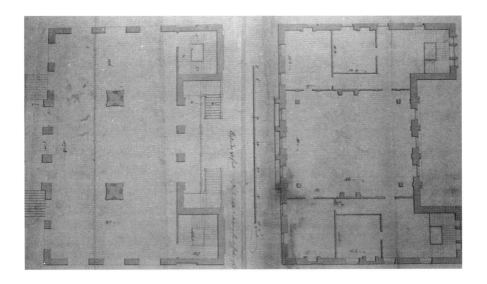

William Rigby Naylor's original floor plans. *Courtesy of the South Carolina Archives.*

Chimney's to be continued from the Foundation to the One pair of Stairs. Floor to be of Bricks Seven Feet Square, and to be finished with Niches Wood Pilasters and good Portland Stone Plinths and Bases, and over each Pier to be one stack of Chimneys…The Piazza fifteen feet in the clear from the Stone Pavement to the Ceiling, the Piazza Floor to be paved with good Purbeck Stone…The Covering of the Roof to be of Welch Carnarvan Slate. The Roof of the Cupelo and the Bed of the Entablature to be covered with Lead…The Doors to the Cellars to be made very strong of Cypress, The Windows to have Iron Bars and Shutters the inside of the same.[94]

At least one of the Horlbecks traveled to England under instruction to obtain the finest materials. The *South Carolina Gazette* reported on January 26, 1769, "Last Thursday evening arrived, in the brigatine Jolleff…a large quantity of portland stone for the new Exchange in this town, with Mr. John Horlbeck, one of the contractors for building that edifice. This is the third importation of this kind for that work."

Thus location, ornamentation, stature and materials all contribute to the grandest product of the American exchange-town hall genre. Architectural historian John M. Bryan states, "In short, having adopted English building types, the Charlestonians attempted to meet English standards of

Charleston's Old Exchange Building

Detail of an engraving by Samuel Smith, based on the painting of Thomas Leitch, showing the Exchange Building. *Courtesy of the Museum of Early Southern Decorative Arts, Winston-Salem, North Carolina.*

construction. In this, of course, the Charleston Exchange is exceptional in the colonies."[95]

Two hundred years previously, a surprisingly similar statement appeared in the *South Carolina Gazette* of January 1771: "We are told that the Custom House and new Exchange, which is allowed to be one of the most elegant structures in America will be finished in May, next."

Perhaps the preeminent meeting of form and function for the grand Exchange came during George Washington's visit. On Saturday, May 7, 1791, the merchants of Charleston sponsored a gathering in President Washington's honor at Charleston's commercial center.

On Saturday, the 7th. instant, sumptuous entertainment was given by the merchants of this city to the president of the united states, in the exchange, at which were present, by invitation, his excellency the governor, his honor the lieutenant governor, the senators and representatives of this state in congress, his honor the intendant, the wardens, with the federal, state, and city officers, all the members of both houses of assembly for Charleston district who were in town, the clergy of every denomination, and many respectable strangers.

They assembled to the number of upwards of three hundred, in the city-hall; on the presidents arrival the ship America, of this place, (being moored off the exchange) fired a federal salute. About half past four the company sat down to an elegant dinner, which was furnished with every delicacy that the country and season could afford. The wines were excellent and in great variety.[96]

After dinner, numerous toasts were given, over fifteen of which were listed in the paper. Particularly noteworthy was the toast spoken by the president to "The commercial interest of Charleston." The newspaper continues:

> *At eight o'clock the president retired to the city-hall, from whence he had a view of fireworks displayed on board the ship, which was illuminated with lanthorns, amidst them the letters V.W.* [Vivat Washington—Long live Washington] *were strikingly conspicuous.*
>
> *The walls of the exchange were beautifully decorated with flowers and shrubs; wreaths of laural encircling the arches; over the presidents seat was exhibited an emblematical painting, representing commerce distributing plenty over the globe. Opposite, under the center arch, was suspended a ship in miniature, handsomely decorated, and furnished with lamps to the number of one hundred and thirty six, which in the evening were lighted up; this at once discovered a beautiful emblematical figure, and formed a most happy substitute for a brilliant chandelier; on her stern was painted "The Commerce of Charleston"; and the repeated acclamations of the company testified to their wishes for her success.*
>
> *The harmony and hilarity which prevailed throughout, were strongly demonstrative of the general gratitude and joy; and it must have afforded the highest gratification to every true patriot, to have observed the man whom we most venerate-venerated by all.*[97]

Over the years some of the grandeur of the original building was lost to modifications, time and natural disasters.[98] Its nobility was diminished when the stair towers were removed from the western façade to accomplish better traffic flow on East Bay Street.[99]

The east side also lost prominence as fill accumulated along the Cooper River and buildings were constructed around the Exchange. The platform or uncovered porch on the east side was removed, though it is unclear exactly when. Here lies another mystery: William Rigby Naylor's plans called for the east porch to be eight feet, six inches wide with steps of the same width on each end of the porch. A plat from 1787 shows steps on each end of the porch;[100] an 1817 plat,[101] however, shows the porch to be twelve feet, four inches wide with the steps missing. A plat from 1837[102] indicates that both the porch and steps were gone. Dr. Elaine Herold's archaeological research found evidence to support the platform width of the 1817 plat.

Was Naylor's 1766 drawing altered during construction, or was the east porch widened before 1817? This question is not yet answered, but Dr.

Herold's findings argue for the notion that the original plan was modified during construction.[103] Hopefully, more information will be found to explain why and when the Exchange lost this important part of its eastern face.

The open arcade of the first floor was gradually enclosed. Robert Mills noted in 1826 that the first floor is "Opened all around…with an arcade forming a spacious, airy walk or change within for the merchants."[104] But Jacob Schirmer's diary entry of September 19, 1835, read: "Custom House commenced filling up the arches of the north end to make a reading room for the Courier Office." [105]

It is thought that the wooden railings in the arches were replaced by iron in 1801.[106] Iron railing was used in the front, but this seems to have been a problem through the years. In December 1846, Schirmer noted in his diary that "This month a new iron railing in front of the Exchange, the relaying of the Flag stone in and outside done by the Walkers was commended in February last." On March 5, 1879, however, he wrote: "Commenced taking down the iron railing in front of the steps going to lay a stone flag pavement and other improvements." On May 11, 1879, Schirmer noted: "New iron railing put up in front of the Post Office, the building has been renovated, some of the offices removed up stairs."

The cupola on the Exchange today is its third. The original contract specified "A cupelo in the Center of the Building with four Venetian Windows and eight Columns of the Ionick Order." Why and when this cupola was removed is not clear. In July 1817, Horlbeck's son, writing to Mr. Theus, collector of the port of Charleston, says, "The Cupola has been

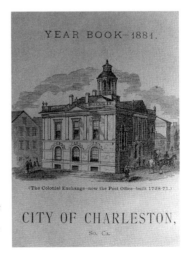

This engraving from the *City of Charleston Yearbook—1881* shows the second cupola. *Courtesy of the Charleston Library Society.*

taken down many years since."[107] Beatrice St. Julien Ravenel, in *Architects of Charleston*, says that the original cupola was wrecked by a storm.

In 1835, a cupola designed by Charles Fraser and built by J.H. Seyle and Albert Elfe was placed on the Exchange at the request of city merchants. This cupola was not only decorative; it was also used as an observatory for ships and a platform from which flag signals were sent. Not everyone was pleased with the appearance of Fraser's cupola. William Gilmore Simms, writing for *Harper's*, said, "The cupola…was stuck on, a sort of pepper box on a terrapin's back."[108]

Many writers link the demise of Fraser's cupola with the earthquake of 1886. This is logical, but wrong. *Charleston, South Carolina in 1883*, printed by Heliotype Printing Company of Boston in 1883, said, "The cupola, which surmounted the roof, having fallen into decay, was removed a short time ago, and the appearance of the building has been much injured in consequence." The heliotype that accompanies the article clearly shows the cupola gone. In *Charleston in 1885*, Arthur Mazyck reported, "Recently, the roof being much out of repair, the cupola and some of the ornamental work have been removed." The Exchange then remained without a crown until the restoration in 1979. The present cupola does not follow the design of either of the previous ornaments.

After the earthquake of 1886, the Exchange Building was propped up with timbers. *Courtesy of the Charleston Museum.*

One thorough overhaul and repair in 1843 appears to have put the building in good condition until the beginning of the Civil War.[109] Unfortunately, along with so much of the city, war damage to the building required more repairs in 1870.

The next great destruction came with the earthquake of 1886. According to a newspaper account, "The Post Office is so badly damaged that examining engineers have advised removal, but it has been temporarily placed in a safe condition by props, Etc."[110] Once more the old Exchange required repair.

When the Light House Service took over the building in 1898, it had been vacant for some time. A remodeling program was begun in 1898 and completed in 1902 at a cost of over $8,000. The crew of the tender *Pharos* helped with free labor. They reworked the plaster and updated the plumbing. The entire floor of the second story was replaced. Partitions were added, window sashes were renewed and a new roof, including new rafters, was built. A stairway leading from the first to the second floor was constructed on the interior. Nothing was done to the outside walls.[111]

Much later, in 1942, "Coast Guard craftsmen had carefully painted the jet black face and the gold marking of the clock [facing Broad Street] as one of their first steps in general fix-up on the building."[112]

His Royal Highness Prince Charles of England spoke at a banquet held in the Great Hall of the Old Exchange in February of 1990. *Photograph courtesy of the Old Exchange.*

Charleston's Old Exchange Building

The Old Exchange after the 1979–1981 restoration. *Sketch by Hector McNeill, courtesy of Rebekah A. McNeill.*

Having gone through two wars, an earthquake and numerous changes and preservation efforts, it is no wonder the once "noble appearance" that greeted Josiah Quincy in 1773 had changed. The Old Exchange and Provost Dungeon museum opened in 1981; the building restored to a semblance of its former grandeur.

The restoration is a modern adaptation of a historic structure, rather than a meticulous rendering of the original Exchange. Iron railings, not the original stone ones, face Broad Street. The stairwells are returned, but to the opposite side of the building, where they allow for an elevator.

Today, one may rent the reproduced Great Hall where Washington was entertained so elegantly and so often. Although much of the woodwork is conjectural, the specifics of the original contract, such as the columns and pine flooring, were followed during the restoration. Adjoining the fine meeting room, which the Great Hall recreates, is a modern catering kitchen. Climate control, with air conditioning as well as heating, has replaced the fireplaces and open arcades. Modern recessed lighting supplements the candlelight.

The Old Exchange and Provost Dungeon is now open as a museum during the day with guided tours. Truly a living building, the structure continues to serve as a tie to the past while being of use to the present.

Notes

1. Register Mesne Conveyance (RMC) Office, Charleston, South Carolina, Book W, 211–213.

2. Ibid., 211–212.

3. Peppercorn rent is a terminology dating back to the Middle Ages. The nominal amount, a single peppercorn served as a token and sealed an agreement. In this case, the lease was in effect until the payment of 800 current pounds by Ebenezer Simmons.

4. RMC Office, Book W, 214–215.

5. Ibid., H-3, 512. The spelling of Simmons varies in the deed. Simmons and Simons are used interchangeably.

6. There were two important two-story buildings in early Charles Town, which are often confused. The Court of Guard, sometimes called Palace at Arms, held "The Council Chamber above, and Guard House below." The other building held "The Court House above and Exchange below." This was early in the eighteenth century. The "Exchange" moved to the first floor of the Exchange Building in 1771.

7. John G. Leland, *Stede Bonnet* (Charleston, South Carolina: Charleston Reproductions, 1972); Douglas Botting, *The Pirates* (Alexandria, Virginia: Time-Life Books, 1978). Most information on pirates originates in *A General History of the Robberies and Murders of the most Notorious Pyrates*, published in 1726. The author is generally recognized as Daniel Defoe writing under a pseudonym.

8. James H. Dorman, *Theater in the Ante-Bellum South* (Chapel Hill, North Carolina: University of North Carolina Press, 1967), 4.

9. *South Carolina Gazette*, February 17, 1733.

10. Dr. Prioleau is quoted from David Ramsay's *History of South Carolina*, vol. 2, 1670–1808, published and sold by W.J. Duffie, 1858. The material from Prioleau appears in a footnote on pages 179–182, which gives the original source as the journal of the Medical Society of South Carolina. Since the journal has disappeared, we owe Ramsay's footnote for the partial preservation of Dr. Prioleau's study. Both men were active members of the medical society, which explains their association. In searching for the Prioleau original, the authors found only an entry in the Minute Book of the Medical Society of South Carolina. At the meeting on October 3, 1805, is recorded "The Vice President [Dr. Prioleau] read to the Society an account of the Hurricanes which occurred in Charleston in the years 1752 and 1804 which was ordered to be sent into circulation." At Dr. Prioleau's death, friends noted his "authority upon any point of fact is indisputable" and "it is to be regretted that he preserved so little in writing."

11. Ibid., 180.

12. Ibid.

13. Elaine B. Herold, "Archaeological Research at the Exchange Building" (Draft copy, Charleston, South Carolina, 1979–1980,) 65.

14. Ibid.

15. *South Carolina Gazette*, April 13, 1767.

16. *Charleston Year Book of 1898*, 365.

17. David Richardson, "The Volume and Pattern of the English Slave Trade to South Carolina Before 1776" (paper delivered to the Southern Historical Association, 49th Annual Meeting, November 12, 1983).

William Dillwyn, visiting Charles Town in 1772, noted in his diary, "walked in the Evening in the Exchange an Hour." Richard Barry writes of the Exchange in his well-researched biography of John Rutledge. By the time of the Constitutional Convention, Rutledge, who had been president of South Carolina and signed the Constitution, was chancellor of South Carolina. Since the Supreme Court did not exist, Rutledge, the man, was "court of last resort" for all South Carolinians. He spent his mornings rendering decisions, and his afternoons on a downtown bench visiting with "locals."

"In the evening—every evening—he went to the Exchange, at the foot of Broad Street, frequented by factors, merchants, and ship captains who came and went at the rate of two to a dozen daily...Thus the only efficient newsmen of the time were these ship captains; the Exchange was their club; the only outsider among them—except merchants and factors, their employers and partners—was the Chancellor. There, in the evening, he [Rutledge] kept his finger on the pulse of the swiftly changing world outside, just as in the afternoon, at the Corner, chatting with members of the Assembly, planters, travelers, workmen, he kept in touch with the Town and the up-country." Richard Barry, *Mr. Rutledge of South Carolina* (New York: Duell, Sloan and Pearce, 1942), 305–306.

18. *South Carolina Gazette*, December 6, 1773.

19. Ibid. It was from this meeting that David Duncan Wallace, in his *South Carolina: A Short History, 1520–1948*, claims the current legislature of South Carolina "has lineally descended." (Chapel Hill, North Carolina: University of North Carolina Press, 1951), 251.

20. *South Carolina Gazette*, December 27, 1773.

21. Information on tea from Marguerite Steedman, "Charleston's Forgotten Tea Party," *Georgia Review* 21, no. 2 (Summer 1967). Also see Walter J. Fraser, "Tea, Taxes and Temerity," a pamphlet.

22. *South Carolina Gazette*, July 11, 1774.

23. William Moultrie, *Memoirs of the American Revolution*, vol. 2. (New York: printed by David Longworth for the author, 1802), 85.

24. *South Carolina Historical Magazine* 57 (1957): 11.

25. Ibid., 11–12.

26. *South Carolina Historical Magazine* 33 (1932): 3.

27. Ibid. 3–4.

28. Henry J. Kauffman, "Early American Gunsmith 1650–1850," *South Carolina Historical Magazine* 29. (Copy available in the Papers of Gadsden Phillips.)

29. Ibid.

30. Caroline Gilman, ed., *Letters of Eliza Wilkinson* (New York, 1839; Reprinted, New York: New York Times & Arno Press, 1969), 88–89. Reprint.

31. Ibid., 93.

32. Address delivered at the seventeenth anniversary of the Black Oak Agricultural Society on Tuesday, April 27, 1858, by Samuel Debose, Esq. A copy with handwritten notation is in the files of the Exchange.

33. Letter from William Edward Hayne, December 23, 1835. Original located in the South Caroliniana Library, Columbia, South Carolina.

34. David Ramsay, *History of the Revolution, vol. II*, 283–284, as quoted in David K. Bowden, *The Execution of Isaac Hayne* (Lexington, South Carolina: The Sandlapper Store, 1977).

35. All Hayne information from David K. Bowden, as cited above.

36. *South Carolina Historical Magazine* 58 (1957): 16.

37. *The Statutes at Large of South Carolina, Volume Seventh, Containing the Acts Relating to Charleston, Courts, Slaves, and Rivers*. Edited under authority of the legislature, by David J. McCord. (Columbia, South Carolina: A.S. Johnston, 1840), 99–100; Statues at Large of South Carolina, Act to Incorporate Charleston. Signed, "In the Senate House, the 13th. day of August, 1783, and in the eighth year of the independence of the United

States of America," by John Lloyd, president of the Senate, and Hugh Rutledge, speaker of the House of Representatives.

38. Ibid., Article IX.

39. Richard Walsh, ed., *The Writings of Christopher Gadsden 1746–1805* (Columbia, South Carolina: University of South Carolina Press, 1966), 265.

40. Charles Fraser, *Reminiscences of Charleston* (Charleston, South Carolina: John Russell, 1854), 45.

41. *News and Courier*, May 5, 1956. Inspection Square is known as Marion Square today.

42. *State Gazette*, March 28, 1785.

43. *Charleston Year Book, 1883*, 503–505. Since references of the time label the first floor as the exchange and second floor city hall, entries in the yearbook lead the authors to believe the president dined on the arcade level and danced upstairs. The dinner was catered by Mr. Williams of the Coffee House. The council ordered "the Exchange be suitably fitted up with Tables, Chairs, Benches, Sconces and Awnings." For the ball on the following night, council "Further recommended that the City Hall be put in Proper order." Note the distinct references to Exchange and City Hall.

44. James A. Hoskins, trans., *President Washington's Diaries, 1791–1799* (Summerfield, North Carolina, 1921).

45. The *City Gazette* or the *Daily Advertiser*, Charleston, May 5, 1791. At the time this newspaper was written, a transparency was something that let light pass through, much like the photographic slides that we call transparencies today. However, the transparencies of the eighteenth century were large banners of gauze, silk or other translucent material. A picture, inscription or design on the fabric became visible when a light was held behind it.

46. *City Gazette*, Friday, May 6, 1791.

47. Hoskins, *President Washington's Diaries*, 28–29.

48. Fraser, *Reminiscences of Charleston*.

49. Ibid.

50. *Directory for the District of Charleston* (Collected by Richard Harbowski, 1809), 113.

51. Abraham Botte, *Charleston Directory and Stranger's Guide* (Charleston, South Carolina, 1816), 17–18.

52. RMC Office, Book W-8, 43.

53. Driver was a term for the senior slave on a plantation. Drivers were responsible for the management of other slaves. Generally chosen early in life and well educated, the driver was given many privileges not accorded other slaves, such as a bigger house and a horse. Drivers were authorized to carry whips as symbols of authority.

54. Captain Basil Hall, Royal Navy, *Travels in North America in the Years 1827 and 1828* (Philadelphia: Carey, Lea, and Carey, 1829), 2:191–193.

55. Henry H. Welch, "The Postal History of Charleston, S.C." *Weekly Philatelic Gossip*, December 13, 1947, 468–470. This article also shows some examples of handstamps.

56. *The Charleston News*, January 11, 1875.

57. Postal information, unless otherwise designated, is from the personal files of Mr. J.V. Nielsen, Charleston, South Carolina.

58. *The Charleston Mercury*, July 30, 1835.

59. Ibid., July 31, 1835.

60. *Charleston Courier*, July 31, 1835.

61. This area is called Marion Square today.

62. Samuel G. Stoney, "Local Lore," *Charleston Evening Post*, March 9, 1952.

63. *Charleston Daily Courier*, August 26, 1863.

64. Robert P. Stockton, "Do You Know Your Charleston?" *Charleston News and Courier*, June 7, 1982. The Charleston chamber of commerce officially recommended to Congress that the Exchange be restored to its original function and turned over to the local merchants. The chamber of commerce wanted to lease the building, restore it and use it as a merchants' exchange.

65. James Truslow Adams, ed., *Dictionary of American History* (New York: Charles Scribner's Sons, 1976), 5:221.

66. In 1898, the DAR's dedicated regent, Mrs. Francis Mather Jones, appointed Mrs. Lee C. Harby to make an effort to secure the Exchange as a gift from the United States government to be held by the Chapter as a historical memorial. Mrs. Harby was succeeding in her first efforts until the mayor of Charleston attempted to procure the building for city use. At that time, she abandoned her efforts. The city's plans fell through, however, and the federal government retained ownership. The building then continued under the Light House Service.

67. "Mrs. George F. VonKolnitz, Regent of the Chapter, appointed the following committee: Mrs. Lee C. Harby, Chairman, Mrs. J. S. Bird, Mrs. William Ogilvie, Mrs. J. C. Simonds, Mrs. C. B. Huiet, Mrs. John A. Hertz, Mrs. G. F. VonKolnitz, exofficio." William Way, *The Old Exchange and Custom House* (Charleston, South Carolina, 1921), 18–19.

68. RMC Office, Book U-24, 591, registered April 20, 1917.

69. Newspaper article found in the vertical files of the Charleston County Library.

70. All material on the silver comes from the files, "Battleship Silver," in possession of the South Carolina Daughters of the American Revolution.

71. Over the years, the Chapter worked diligently to preserve the Exchange. The organization also showed their concern for community and country. During the Great Depression, when the Works Progress Administration hired seamstresses to make clothes for the needy, six members of the Rebecca Motte Chapter volunteered to cut material each week in the room of the Exchange now known as the State Daughters of the American Revolution Room. Other community projects include a $500 college scholarship each year

to a student who graduates from Tamassee, a private, non-profit school in upper South Carolina totally supported by the National Society Daughters of the American Revolution for children in need. The Tamassee school was begun by the State DAR in 1919.

The Chapter has worked to place historic markers throughout Charleston. Patriotism is encouraged by awarding R.O.T.C. medals at Charleston Southern University, The Citadel and the College of Charleston. History essay contests and Good Citizenship Awards are given in local high schools to promote awareness of America's heritage. The DAR supplies study manuals to foreign citizens seeking American citizenship. Finally, the Chapter's concern for historic preservation and awareness reaches to Washington, D.C., with donations of money for a Period Room. These Period Rooms, located in the headquarters building of the DAR in Washington, D.C., are furnished by several of the states' chapters. The South Carolina Period Room is a bedroom furnished in the style of the early 1800s.

72. *Charleston Evening Post*, November 26, 1924.

73. John Miller had been employed for the Brunswick Town project and worked under the direction of Stanley South of the University of South Carolina.

74. These artifacts belong to the Rebecca Motte Chapter of the DAR and were exhibited by the Charleston Museum and the Provost Museum.

75. The official report is on file in the Exchange Building.

76. The information on the participation of C. Harrington Bissell and Thomas E. Thornhill in the Provost Museum was obtained from records on file in the Exchange Building and personal interviews with Mr. Bissell.

77. The commission originally consisted of eleven persons, but the act was amended in 1977 to have twelve members on the commission. It was composed of three members elected by the House and Senate in joint assembly; two members of the Rebecca Motte Chapter of the DAR; two members of the State Society of the DAR; the attorney general; the chairman of the South Carolina Parks, Recreation and Tourism Commission or his designee; and the chairman of the South Carolina Department of Archives and History Commission or his designee as non-voting members; a voting member of the Senate; and a voting member of the House. Members of the Old Exchange Building Commission during restoration were: Hugh Z. Graham Jr., chairman; Armine Kingsland Richardson, vice-chairman; John E. Hills, secretary-treasurer; Charles L. Anger; Louise Turner Burgdorf; Joyce Howard Ellis; Victor S. Evans; Representative Sam P. Manning; Nancy Gary Pinckney; Charles Pinckney Roberts; Senator Thomas E. Smith Jr.; and Mary Elizabeth Davenport Vaughn.

78. RMC Office, Book P-115, 35, filed September 16, 1977.

79. Copies of the contracts are on file in the Exchange Building.

80. Architectural restoration information comes from interviews with Mr. Mitchell conducted by the authors.

81. The opening ceremony began with a grand parade on Broad Street and continued in front of the Exchange Building. Governor Richard W. Riley Jr., U.S. Energy Secretary James B. Edwards and Superintendent of Independence National Historic Park Hobart G. Cawood spoke at the historic occasion. Edwards said the building is " a symbol of freedom for all mankind."

82. John M. Bryan, "A Most Noble Appearance" *View of Architecture* (South Carolina Chapter of the American Institute of Architects, 1975): 26–30.

83. John Burchard and Albert Bush-Brown, T*he Architecture of America, A Social and Cultural History* (New York: Little, Brown, and Company, 1961), 65.

84. Andrea Palladio, *The Architecture of A. Palladio*, "In four Books, Revis'd, Design'd and Publish'd by Giacomo Leoni, a Venetian…Translated from the Italian Original," as quoted in William A. Coles, and Henry Hope Reed Jr., eds., *Architecture in America: A Battle of Styles* (New York: Appleton-Century-Crofts, Inc., 1961), 11–13.

85. Christopher Wren, *Of Architecture and Observations on Antique Temples*, as quoted Ibid., 14.

86. From the notes of Albert Simons, F.A.I.A., on file in the office of Mitchell, Small, Donahue, and Logan, Architects.

87. Journal of Josiah Quincy Jr., 1773, published in *Proceedings of the Massachusetts Historical Society* 49 (June 1916): 440–441.

88. Leitch's engraving is in the collection of the Museum of Early Southern Decorative Arts in Winston-Salem, North Carolina.

89. Mason's drawing is pictured in Alice R. Huger Smith, *The Dwelling Houses of Charleston, S.C.* (Philadelphia: J.B. Lippincott Co., 1917).

90. *South Carolina Gazette and Country Journal*, October 19, 1773.

91. A copy is on file in the Exchange Building.

92. Beatrice St. Julien Ravenel, *Architects of Charleston* (Charleston, South Carolina: Carolina Art Association, 1964), 38; E. Milby Burton, *Charleston Furniture 1700–1825* (Columbia, South Carolina: University of South Carolina Press, 1971), 132.

93. Gene Waddell to the authors, February 13, 1983.

94. *Charleston Year Book of 1898.*

95. Bryan, "A Most Noble Appearance," 28.

96. *The Charleston City Gazette*, Tuesday, May 10, 1791.

97. Ibid.

98. In *Southern Tour*, or *Second Series of the Black Book*, vol. 11 (Washington, 1831), 22–23, writer Anne Royall states: "The Exchange is neither very large nor handsome."

99. *City Gazette and Daily Advertiser*, August 16, 1800: "Persons willing to contract for the making of the repairs and alterations in the Exchange, are requested to send in their proposals in writing, sealed, to either of the subscribers by ten o'clock on Tuesday next, viz: to take down the wings, steps, etc., the windows, cornice and pillars to present the

same appearance in the front of the building as they now do.

"To board and slate the roof and repair the same where necessary, continuing the parapet wall, the floor of it to be leaded over, and the gutters of the pediments repaired so as to make the whole sound and tight.

"To erect a single flight of steps to enter into the center arch, opposite to Broad Street, to project into the street so far as not to require more than two steps to be cut in the arch at the leading place, with an iron railing on each side thereof.

"To erect two flights of stairs within the blank space of walls on the west side, at the north and south ends agreeable to a plan in the hands of the subscribers. To fix up a light iron ceiling within such of the arches as at present remain open. The whole of the building with-out to be rough cast." (Singed, Wm. Smith E. Coffin Wm. Lee, Jr. Committee of repairs of the Exchange.)

It was twenty-two years earlier that Ebenezer Hazard, a surveyor of the post roads, was sent to the Southern seaboard. His mission was to investigate and improve postal communications. He reports on Charleston, "January 30th. Cloudy weather and rain. Dined with Peter Bounetheau, Esqr. The exchange, state house, St. Michael's Church, and the new church, are large, brick buildings, rough-cast."

Quoted from "A View of Coastal South Carolina in 1778: The Journal of Ebenezer Hazard," edited by H. Roy Merrens, in the *South Carolina Historical Magazine* 73 (1972): 183. The manuscript journal of Ebenezer Hazard is in the possession of the Historical Society of Pennsylvania.

100. RMC Office, Book A-8, 4.

101. Ibid., Book W-8, 431.

102. Ibid., Book W-10, 598.

103. Dr. Elaine Herold's complete report is on file at the exchange Building.

104. Robert Mills, *Statistics of South Carolina* (Charleston, South Carolina, 1826; Spartanburg, South Carolina: The Reprint Company, 1972), 407–408.

105. All quotes from the Schirmer Diary are taken from the original, on file at the South Carolina Historical Society.

106. *City Gazette and Daily Advertiser*, August 16, 1800, 6.

107. Way, *Old Exchange and Custom House*, 6.

108. William Gilmore Simms, "Charleston: the Palmetto City," *Harper's New Monthly Magazine* 15, no. 85 (June 1857).

109. *Charleston Year Book of 1898*, 361.

110. "Charleston As It Is After the Earthquake Shock of August 31, 1886," Charleston newspaper accounts, 1886.

111. Charleston newspaper article of March 1933, on file at the Charleston Public Library.

112. *Charleston News and Courier*, December 31, 1942.

Index

Prison Ship 32
Pritchard, Sheriff 32
Provost 31, 32, 33, 34, 35, 36
Provost Dungeon 65, 69, 82

Q
Quincy, Josiah, Jr. 73, 82

R
Ramsay, Doctor David 32, 40
Rathbun, Ted A. 65
Rawdon, Lord 34
Rhett, William 16
Robinson, Emmett 65
Rutledge, Edward 32
Rutledge, John 29, 61

S
Sarazen, sisters 33
Savage, John 13
Schirmer, Jacob 79
Simmons, Ebenezar 13
Simms, William Gilmore 80
Simons, Mitchell, Small and Donahue
        66
Sinkler, Peter 34
slave trade 22, 23, 41, 42, 49
   slave auction description 49–51
Smith, Josiah 32
Stark, Colonel 31
Stevens, Daniel 31, 36, 37

T
taxes 21, 25
   customs & duties 22, 25, 42, 57, 58,
        73
Tea Act 25
tea controversy 25, 27, 28

theatre 18, 43, 44
Thornhill, Thomas E. 64
Timothy, Peter 32
Trumbo, Christopher 57

V
Vauban 11

W
Waddell, Gene 74
Walker, Evans and Cogswell 56
Washington, George 28, 42, 44, 45, 46,
        47, 63, 69, 76, 78
Wilkinson, Eliza 33
Woodin, Thomas 74
World War I 60
World War II 60, 61
Wren, Sir Christopher 72

About the Authors

Ruth M. Miller is a graduate of Duke University and a former high school teacher. A licensed city guide and local historian since 1979, she co-founded Charleston Strolls, a tour service for Charleston and the Carolina Lowcountry. She is the company's current owner.

Ruth is the author and illustrator of *Charleston Charlie*, and co-author of *The Angel Oak Story: John's Island Reminiscences*.

Ann Taylor Andrus, a native of North Carolina, is a graduate of the University of North Carolina, Chapel Hill, School of Dental Hygiene. She became a registered historic tour guide for Charleston in 1979, and, with Ruth Miller, co-founded Charleston Strolls.

Ann is recognized as a local Methodist Church historian and is the author of *The Name Shall Be Bethel*, published in 1997.